# Igniting
# Greatness

To your Greatness! Hala!

# Igniting
by Howard Glasser
with Melissa Lowenstein
# Greatness

*Remembering who
we really are through the
Nurtured Heart Approach®*

This book is dedicated to the greatness of your heart:

Breathe with your heart
Then see, hear, speak, touch, feel and taste
With your heart
And
Your Heart will generate endless experiences
And explorations
Of love and joy.

# Acknowledgements

I wish to thank all those who have supported the work of the Nurtured Heart Approach with great dedication. I am honored by your continued desire to help children, families and communities through this noble work. I am also in great appreciation of the Children's Success Foundation for multiplying the reach of this approach that now impacts so many adults as well.

I also wish to thank those who agreed to be readers for this particular project: Jan Hunter, Tanya Frazier, Celeste Elsey, Veronica Coates, and Josh Kuersten. I value your time, veracity and expression in reviewing this book and in lending yourself to the momentum I needed to move it to completion. Thanks to my friend Moises for inspiration.

Thank you so much to Owen DeLeon of Owen Visual Communications. Both your talent and your amazing attitude of collaboration on the book cover and the book design are so appreciated.

I want to expressly appreciate my daughter Alice Glasser, who has emerged as not only my foundational support in all matters involving art and design, but now, in life itself. You have continued to inspire me; and, more than ever, you purposefully motivate me to greater greatness than I ever thought possible. I am so grateful.

Lastly, I want to thank my dear friend, colleague, and collaborator, Melissa Lynn Lowenstein (formerly Block). It would be unfair to say that Melissa makes my work as an author easy, because every new project requires blood, sweat and tears; but I can say that she makes the process of writing amazingly accessible, simple and welcoming. I unendingly look forward to working with her. She embodies the spirit of the muse; her encouragement and excitement infinitely motivate and inspire our best, most revealing, and inspiring work. It is an absolute pleasure to work with her, and my appreciation is abundant.

- Howard Glasser

Thanks to my wonderful tribe: a community of awakened, peaceful, passionate, hilarious, embodied human beings! Thanks to my children, Sarah and Noah, for the privilege of mothering you and witnessing your unfolding greatness. You're my best teachers. And thanks to William, my superhero-like long-time friend and now life partner, for jumping in with me, and for sharing with me your beautiful son Kai.

My biggest gratitude goes to Howard Glasser for entrusting me with his vision as it's set down, word by word, on the pages we create together. It is an enormous gift to me as a writer to be able to apply my skill and insight to promote a movement that helps so many. To collaborate on this book, directed at adults who wish to maximize their own happiness and achievement through the Nurtured Heart Approach – our seventh together! – was an honor and a pleasure. I'm inspired by Howard's determination, courage, and joyous spirit, and I hope we never run out of books to write together!

- Melissa Lowenstein

# Table of Contents

Table of Contents

This book is intended to support readers in a journey of self-help and self-discovery. It will not and is not intended to take the place of professional psychotherapy.

# Foreword

No definitive book on greatness can be written, because it has no end. It is, and always will be, a realm of exploration, open to the vast possibilities of what we can imagine now and have yet to imagine.

I can imagine nothing more satisfying than exploring into the farthest reaches of greatness. The more I allow myself to push into this exploration, the more greatness comes. Pouring my own energy in that direction brings splendor into form, bringing waves and pulsations of inspiration and manifestation into the constructs of the everyday.

We are carving a path for future generations. In learning and living the work of greatness, we show others what is possible. We inspire others to awaken to the great mystery of life and light up the runway to more: more people dedicated to the lone path of trusting their unique dreams and living their unique purposes, perhaps despite all odds; and more people dancing to the source energy of inspiration, trusting their heart's desires as their guides. Those who risk this exploration are being cheered on and energized every step of the way by the benevolent universe, which cherishes and relishes the beauty and significance of all that unfolds as a result.

Greatness is in our birthright and in our hardware. This surprises many people as they begin their journey of awakening their greatness. For years, I've keenly watched this unfolding occur as people recognize that they signed up for greatness as a soul before even gaining the privilege and honor of being born into existence. In the process, however, they may come to see how they've also brilliantly designed a scenario of characters and circumstances constructed to challenge and test that greatness to the hilt. Although we design our destinies of greatness, challenges are part of that design.

Imagine zillions of souls out in the ethers somewhere, waiting and wanting to get a body in which to live another life. Now, imagine that a celestial review committee is responsible for choosing which souls get this privilege. Called before the panel, souls might be challenged: "Well…you forgot your greatness last time. How are you going to remember it this time around?"

A soul might lobby back with scenarios where challenges might arise, and insist to the panel that they would still remain in their greatness. "My family will tell me how stupid I am. My teachers and fellow students will make me feel silly and dumb. This time, I will remember the greatness of my intelligence." Zoom and plop, into a body she'd go, and these challenges would crop up to test her resolve during this trip through a lifetime.

The challenges we *think* we face are *self-improvement, boosting self-esteem,* maybe being a higher achiever, competing better in the rat race of life, improving relationships with specific people in our lives, or finding the relationship, livelihood or self-definition that might make us feel just *okay* about who we are. **The true challenge we came to meet was that of simply remembering the greatness we brought with us into this world: not only remembering it, but doing so with verve, and doing so again and again, until greatness choruses drown out the old critical cacophony that restrains us from living out who we really are.**

Yes, this is a process of remembering: remembering your soul's purpose, dream and desire. It is not limited to high-water marks of accomplishment and record-breaking feats. It is about living out the unique constellation of your soul's splendor in the form of qualities of greatness that activate your life in ways that will surprise and delight you.

This book is about how, first, to remember your greatness; and, second, to take purposeful next steps of igniting that greatness and fanning its flames. It is an examination of the ways in which one can shift to seeing and being in greatness, to the benefit of herself and every person her life touches. It is about a path to love. Ultimately, this is what the work described in this book teaches: an actualization of love for others and for one's self.

I'm reminded of the final days of a training I gave for educators at the Sallie B. Howard School for the Performing Arts in North Carolina, where quite a few participants came to me to thank me directly for "showing them how to love." Several of these trainees went on to explain that they had strong religious faith and had, at the training's outset, grappled with the integration of their faith with what I was teaching. By the end of the week we spent together, they realized that while their religious faith had deeply inspired them to love and to have loving hearts, the methodology of this approach had opened the door to a way of being loving. It guided them to choose love in every communication, directing their actions in a way that felt energetically aligned with that desire to live lives of love.

Many faiths and philosophies recommend being more loving – let's assume that, in their purest form, all do – but they do not necessarily provide tools and methods for *how* to activate this love within the contexts of their thoughts and expressions to self and others. This book and the work to which I have devoted my life offer a way to manifest that love that so pervades our hearts: how to *be* loving in context of relationship. The Nurtured Heart Approach is a greatness practice that amplifies and clarifies the loving natures that have been within us all along but that can so easily become shrouded, convoluted, and energetically incongruent through normal approaches to interrelating.

Great love, great integrity, and other great qualities such as resilience, giving, collaboration, wisdom and power are some of the many magnificent manifestations of splendor that take unique form within you. Although your constellation may contain a host of qualities similar to those of others, it is unlike anyone else's. Your idiosyncratic character, drive and desires fire a distinctive signature and one-of-a-kind inner perspective that only you can know and explore further. The greatness of compassion, kindness, and collaboration that you are enjoying today is the spark; and as you fan the flames, endless resonant dimensions of each quality will reveal themselves in concert with others. They will dance on your behalf and on behalf of others and the world: the perfect win-win-win.

Only you know and can manifest this expansion and unfolding. You can restrain it or entertain it. It is always and entirely your choice. Listen carefully, and you will hear your greatness calling.

To your greatness,
Howard Glasser

# Introduction
## From the Nurtured Heart Approach
## to Greatness Practice: A Brief History

E very adult has, at some point, known a child who seemed addicted to pushing boundaries. Many explanations have been offered to explain the behavior of this kind of child: brain dysfunction, early childhood wounding, unmet developmental needs, parental incompetence, family dysfunction, school stress, poor diet. While all of these elements can play a role in a child's behaviors, none of them has yet been found to tell the whole story.

Back in the 1990s, when I began my therapy practice, I specialized in working with this type of child. I tried complex approaches to help them and their families achieve a more peaceful, successful way of being. My efforts, which were informed by my education as a therapist, often seemed to backfire.

One by one, I moved through every sensible theory and practice I could discern, and one by one they fell away. As I was pretty darn loyal to the methods I studied, I applied them in every creative way I could conjure up before casting them aside as untenable. "If some isn't good enough," I reasoned, "more must be better." With determination, I would ramp up my application of the same strategies...and things would continue to fall apart. I had to admit to myself that I was not helping—that I was, in fact, making things worse for families already in crisis. It felt awful. It certainly gave me great compassion for the families of these children, as they were most often ramping up just like I was – trying their methods as hard as they could.

Eventually I moved into the blessed space of 'not knowing.' Then, through a combination of intuition, divine guidance and what felt like total molecular recall of my own childhood as a challenging child, I began to feel, see and sense *the energy* between family members during each interaction I witnessed in session. I soon saw that the tools I had been using were the wrong ones for the job. I saw that no matter how intensively I used those wrong tools, they would continue to not only to *not* work—just as hammering a nail in with a screwdriver will not work, no matter how hard you hammer – they would systemically make things worse.

My sense of the energy passing between adults and children came to inform everything I did in my therapy practice. Creative ideas began to take over my being in the middle of the night. I marched them into the treatment room and observed how each worked in a variety of situations. Parents sat bolt upright in recognition of the underlying rightness of what I was doing and explaining to them. I began to hear the words, "That makes *so much* sense!" many times each day.

As parents incorporated what I taught them into their parenting and watched their new efforts come to fruition, I got crystal clear about how to work in a way that would benefit even the most difficult child. This led me to develop an approach that brought about rapid turnarounds even in the most challenging children. Other child therapists began to send me their toughest cases.

I would routinely require that each family apply the same principles and practices to their most cooperative children as well – children who often existed in the shadows of their more challenging siblings, who had previously gotten the lion's share of attention from parents. I affectionately referred to those non-challenging siblings as the 'understudies.' They were taking notes, and if they were excluded from this wonderful new way they saw their parents interacting with a sibling who they already often perceived as cheating them of parental connection, they would act out to get their turn as well. I soon saw that the methods that were developing through me could not only quell that pattern, but could also help normal, high-achieving, and great-behaving kids flourish at greater levels than ever.

In its first few years, this approach didn't have a name. It was just the particular work I did in my therapy practice and taught to interns under my tutelage. Then, one day, I remembered an event from a decade and a half earlier. At a meditation retreat, a favorite teacher mentioned that he was trying to name a process he was sharing. I suggested that he name his method the Nurtured Heart Approach. He thought it over, then said, "No – that's the name for *your* approach."

When I had this conversation, I didn't even *have* an approach. I was taking a break from my work as a psychotherapist to pursue interests in art and spiritual practices. I had no idea what he was referring to. Fifteen years later, I had an approach that needed a name, and this one fit.

The primary insight that led me in the building of this approach was that **adults, almost without fail, accidentally give significant relationship and energy to children's poor choices; rarely do they give the same quality or quantity of energy to their child's good choices.** They are trying as hard as they can to do their best parenting with normal, conventional and traditional approaches, and it's those *methods* that are the culprit – because they are laden with energized response when things go wrong.

When one child hits another, the responsible, good-hearted parent or teacher is likely to spend a lot of time talking to the perpetrator about how *we don't hit. It's not nice to hit. Our friends don't feel safe around us when we hit.* It makes everyone feel bad when we hit. Whether the child gets a gentle lecture, a stronger reprimand, or a stern time-out, the end result is that the child gets lively energy, connection and relationship in response to his poor choice.

**Ultimately, the most cherished resource a child accesses is connection with the adults in his life in various forms and degrees of energized relationship.** Long before he can speak or walk, he or she dials in how to access the biggest possible influx of that energy. No wonder children end up confused. They are told to be good, but they get a lot more of what is most important to them when they are bad.

The Nurtured Heart Approach teaches adults to flip **that energy so that the child feels seen, heard and deeply acknowledged when he is not misbehaving.** This entails actively recognizing any available facet of the child's greatness, even in its most emergent and subtle expressions. For example: a child who is playing peacefully with a friend is choosing to not hit. That's the truth of the moment. He is getting along, collaborating, being wise and thoughtful, cooperating and using good judgment. These are all aspects of the child's innate greatness that can be celebrated any time he is not hitting—which, for even the most terrifyingly intense child, is a fair amount of the time.

People who know me well are accustomed to my habit of occasionally making quirky, push-the-envelope kinds of statements. My intensity does love to emerge in that way. I love to see the looks on people's faces as they try to figure out whether I'm serious, and if I am, what on Earth I might really mean. In this tradition, one day not too long ago, someone who didn't know me well asked me what I did for a living, and I joyously blurted, "I'm an arsonist!"

**My work is, at its root, about igniting greatness.** I never get tired of that moment where I see someone catch fire with the potential of intentionally creating and growing greatness in herself and in others.

Susan Redford, a dual-licensed mental health and substance abuse professional, uses the Nurtured Heart Approach in her work with adult women battling drug addiction. The transformations that have occurred in these groups are some of the best examples of the moment where greatness catches fire and sets a course away from problems and toward positivity and success. One of her patients, Sophie, a 19-year-old mother of two young children, had begun using crystal methamphetamine at 13, and had not been able to completely kick the habit. If she failed to complete her Child Protective Services plan, she faced losing custody of her children. In group, Sophie talked about mold that had grown in her apartment. It was making her children sick. She described her efforts to find better housing with her Section Eight grant. Susan said to Sophie, "You have taken your children to the doctor. You are giving them their medicine and you are trying to keep your apartment as clean as possible. You're advocating for your family with your landlord and looking for new housing. I'm a good mother too, and you are doing everything I can think of to try to make a difference for your children…I have to accuse you right now of being a good mother."

Bursting into tears, Sophie shared that no one, not once, not ever, had called her a good mother. "They just tell me I'm a rotten mother because I used drugs, and they tell me I can never be a good mother." But that day, she was seen as already successful, as living out her greatness in important ways, and she was acknowledged for it in a way that felt convincing and real. This was a transformative moment for Sophie. Her greatness, in that very moment, caught fire. Within a month, Sophie had found new housing for her family and her CPS case was closed.

This is only one of many tales of transformation through Susan's work with women who many believed to be beyond help. The stories of Susan's patients resonate with me especially well because in my own youth, I applied my intensity to experimenting with drugs. I did a lot of them, often, and when I consider some of the choices I made then, I'm frankly stunned I made it this far, let alone survived.

Intense people are drawn to this world of substances. It gives a sighting into a glimmer of the sacred: often, by way of heightened glimpses of one's own greatness-nature and the greatness-nature of other people. Substances can help us see 'greatness moments' in context of the world we live in. Of course, finding those moments this way is dangerous, yielding only brief and progressively more elusive positive experiences. The cosmic smack upside the head is that we think we have to go back to the pot or the beer, the wine or the liquor, the LSD or the heroin, the peyote or the cocaine, to return to that sacred space.

In the years following my experimentation with substances, I found that I could alternatively bring more consistent versions of splendor into form through art—specifically, through woodworking, which is what I spent ten years doing after my initial therapist training. I dropped out of graduate school and lived the belief that bringing splendor to form must mean manifesting my next cabinet or wood sculpture. The sculptures, especially, brought me closer to a sense of purpose. Several more years would pass before I realized that my true work involved not wood, but humanity.

The approach that birthed through me in response to families in crisis with challenging children has emerged as capable of reminding people of the sense of love that is intrinsic to the heaven of being human. Although we have not been at a loss for words to express disdain, disappointment, criticism, revulsion, resignation, frustration, and other facets of the negative side of things, we have been at a huge loss for words to describe positive expressions of our loving hearts. This is the space in which I found my true calling.

**This book is my love song to the possibility of energized relationship, connection and experience in the realm of positivity—more precisely, in that realm I call greatness.** It's been my privilege and sacred commitment to be a vital part of developing the language of this realm.

# How to Use
# this Book

This book outlines an approach to life based on an outlook that I hope to convey in a way that you feel in your bones. It will provide you with a methodology and tools you can begin to use right away to change the ways you respond to life internally and the ways you react and respond to others. As you apply this approach, you realize the greatness you already possess. As you put your attention on that greatness, it grows.

The book is divided into three sections: Mind (Theory), Heart (Practice) and Spirit (& Beyond…). These sections reflect a process of transformation that, for most, will go something like this:

Developing a mind-centered grasp of the principle of upside-down energy and the ways we play it out in relationships with ourselves and others

↓

Learning to engage in a heart-centered practice where we apply diligent intention to shift long-held and deep patterning

↓

Expanding into a spiritual arc that takes the practice to new levels

…and there is always potential to go back through the mind, through the heart, and into spirit, winding through these centers from many directions as the journey continues, spiraling into ever-expanding understanding and awakening.

With this in mind, read this book first from start to finish, especially if you are unfamiliar with the Nurtured Heart Approach. This will bring you through the first loop of the spiral. Once that momentum is built, you may want to revisit parts of the book as you continue to explore. The impact of an idea or practice will shift and change each time you touch back into it on your journey.

Part One

# Theory

*All that I am*

*All that I see*

*All that I've been and all that I'll ever be*

*Is a blessing*

*It's so amazing*

*And I'm grateful for it all, for it all*

- from "Grateful," written and performed
  by Nimesh "Nimo" Patel and Daniel Nahmod

*Somewhere, something incredible is waiting to be known.*

- Carl Sagan

# Five Lightning
## Strikes

About the time my first book came out, in the late 1990s, I was running a counseling center, The Tucson Center for the Difficult Child. As we honed and polished the approach I had developed, we were seeing amazing results in the youth and families we served. One clue to me at the time of its impact and power: even novice therapy, counseling and social work interns who learned to use it with our clients were having greater impact than seasoned professionals using more standard models.

And then, due to some administrative goof by our parent network in getting its grant proposal to its funder in time, we lost the majority of the clinic's funding for the next five-year fiscal cycle. The center was forced to fold.

In the wake of the bad news of that error, I woke in a sweat multiple times each night for days on end. I was steeped in fear, misery, doubt, sadness, worry, rage, and panic. One such evening, my inner storm brought me to a series of epiphanies in a manner that felt like bolts of lightning. These bolts of lightning struck in the midst of my profound perseveration on all that was troubling about my emerging situation. Each progressive strike opened me up to what felt like a deeper level of truth.

*Lightning Strike 1:* Although I thought I was a highly positive person, and although teaching radical appreciation was at the heart of my work, I saw with a flash and a jolt that when push came to shove—when the rubber met the road—I was actually a highly negative person. I suddenly and clearly saw that at the core of my being, I was living a lie.

I espoused positivity in my workshops and writings. But when the chips were down, I became nearly overwhelmed with worry, misery, and doubt (my personal WMDs, and the most fundamental weapons of mass destruction – the ones that, at some level, have motivated the creation of every other WMD that now exists on the planet). At that point, I saw with new X-ray vision my own tendency to default to negativity, especially when under pressure.

*Lightning Strike 2:* I had been working with a young man to try to figure out some computer issues I was having, and he made many references to default settings. In a flash of insight, I saw that my thoughts seemed to have actual default settings, just like my computer. When left to its own devices or threatened in any significant way, my mind defaulted to negativity.

*Lightning Strike 3:* This kid Justin, the one who was helping me with my computer, kept insisting on showing me how to change default settings on my machine, and I was a little resistant because I didn't know much about computers. And then, I realized that this negativity was *just* a default setting, and that default settings can change. I could picture the possibility, just as if I were choosing an advanced setting from a remote pull-down menu in my computer's system preferences.

*Lightning Strike 4:* I resolved to shift to a new set of defaults that would enable me to stay with my commitment to positivity, even under difficult circumstances. I saw how simply recognizing the possibility for a shift wouldn't create the shift I wanted; I knew I had to set a clear intention, and that this setting of intention held as much energetic importance as the recognition that a shift was possible.

I didn't need to analyze the old software to understand why it had been there until now, and I didn't need to know why it wasn't working. I could simply download this new software of positivity, and it would overwrite the influence of the old software. I could consciously and intentionally grow the parts of myself I could already identify as positive.

*Lightning Strike 5:* The only method I believed in fully was the Nurtured Heart Approach. In this last lightning bolt of insight, I committed to exploring the impact the approach would have if I applied it on myself—to seeing how far I could take it in my arc of personal growth. I could use the approach I had developed to change those default settings to all that was good and great.

This perfect storm of electrifying bolts left me with a profound and enduring sense of knowing. I've never maintained a resolution with such fierce determination as I have in sustaining this stance; even now, my resolve continues to grow. This was a commitment made in heaven.

I could be my own therapist, just as I could teach a parent to be his or her child's therapist (therapist simply means "agent of change"). I could use the tools of this approach to change the programming in my mind and heart, just as I can upgrade my computer with new downloads to improve its functioning. Some software packages come bundled with wonderful features we might not have sought out but that turn out to be beneficial; and sometimes these "downloads" I experienced carried with them delightful surprises. For reasons I will explain, I have developed vast faith in not only exploring positivity, but in finding next levels of greatness. So often, one leap forward has led to many more.

Just as the air feels clean and vibrant after a lightning storm, I felt clean and vibrant after my own series of insights. I could rest in knowing that I didn't need to wish I could be greater, or more powerful, or more like someone I admired. I could *actively cultivate my own greatness.* And I had already created a map for this exploration: the Nurtured Heart Approach.

# Reframing
## Intensity

When I was in college, sensitivity training groups were just becoming popular, and I joined one. One person I admired said, in front of the whole group, "Howie, you are *really intense.*"

I freaked out. Intense, to me, meant crazy. Dangerous. Frightening. *Too much.* As a grown-up difficult child, I knew well what it felt like to be *too much.* My reaction was, well, intense— because that person was right, I *was* intense. I *am* intense. But my definition of that term has shifted dramatically in the many years that have passed since then.

Intensity is life force. Intensity is power. Intensity is our connectedness to the energy that runs the whole universe, both seen and unseen. Intensity is the way that energy shows up in us and runs through us. It is our greatest gift and carries our greatest potential. It can be directed into greatness and luminosity, or it can go awry and be directed elsewhere, in unproductive ways. Some of us carry more of it than others, but all of us carry it, and all of us choose how it is expressed.

Unless someone is providing wonderful mentoring for us, pointing out for us how our intensity is serving a greater good, it is easy to conclude that intensity is the enemy. The fact that our intensity can pull us into dicey places and situations may lead us to think of it as troubling. Notions of intensity as bad have led our society to systematically medicate away the troubling symptoms of an intense child – something we would never do if we thought intensity was a great gift. Medications can create an illusion of moderated intensity; the message to the child is, "Something is wrong with you because of your intensity. We need to make it go away, because you apparently can't handle it; nor can your parents or teachers."

It's time to take a fresh look at how intensity can be re-connected to excellence – how it is the life force that we need to live in greatness. When seen in this light, it is the last thing we'd want to cover up or push away.

To help you understand the 'energetic' of intensity, I'll share a metaphor I've used for years to convey how kids 'plug in' to energy. With this, I hope to seed the sense that we can reconnect the precious gift of our life force and intensity in ways that promote the acting-out of greatness. If I describe this well enough, you'll not only feel the core of the issue in your bones, you'll have a knowing sense of how to transpose this to the energetics of how you choose to live your life.

What I often share as a way of conveying this basic premise of my work is my belief that we truly are our *children's favorite toys*. Think about how children respond when receiving a new toy. No matter what they may be currently focused on, when given a new toy they will change gears. They'll remove the toy from its packaging and launch into a mode of exploration. Any toy worth purchasing will have at least one compelling feature. Most toys have a host of features, whether two or two hundred thousand.

When a child happens upon a feature that bores or fails to compel him, he takes note. He may return a few times, either accidentally or on purpose, to see whether the feature gets more interesting. Once he sees the truth of its relative 'boringness,' however, he'll ditch it in favor of the toy's more intriguing features.

Now how about us as 'toys' for the children in our lives? How many features do *we* have? Even if we are to some extent physically limited, we can still move in an infinite variety of ways. Combine that flexibility with our huge array of moods and emotions – all our ways of getting animated, excited, depressed, or frustrated, all with our very own personal, idiosyncratic nuances – and we win, hands down, as the most fascinating toy in our child's toy collection. We are actually the best entertainment center imaginable.

Therein lies the energetic dilemma that eventually migrates to the space between our very own ears. Even though intensity, sensitivity, and neediness can all ultimately be great gifts to inspired lives—gifts that help us to manage and gauge our forays into our endeavors – show me a child who is a little more intense than the next kid, along with being a little more sensitive and a little more needy, and I'll show you a child who winds up running headlong into a corridor of life that gets to be exceedingly non-entertaining.

For example, put a child like that into a home or classroom conducted or organized around the principles and practices of normal, traditional, and conventional parenting and teaching, and I'll show you a child who drinks in 'energetically upside-down' impressions of how the world works and their impact in those environments.

When they do the right things, we 'toys' are energetically pale. We're not expressive. When they make poor choices, we don't only show up 100 percent of the time; *we really show up* with highly energetic responses. Over time, the child forms an *energetic impression* that these toys (the adults in their lives) are more interesting and compelling when things are going wrong. This is a life-changing conclusion for the child. It leads them to ditch even bothering doing the right thing. The adults in their worlds are so much more boring when they follow the rules.

Here, now, is how this transposes to how we adults live our lives. If this 'software' I inadvertently 'downloaded' has governed my thoughts and actions since early childhood, this same dynamic is likely to continue to govern my interactions with others as well as my internal interactions with myself.

Having learned this in childhood, we tend to carry it into adulthood by giving skimpy, energetically pale airtime to the good things we do and the good choices we make. At the same time, we tend to fall over and over again into the perpetuating trap of highly energized internal thoughts surrounding poor choices and generalized negativity. We think nothing of endlessly perseverating on these downward-spiraling thoughts. Indeed, this dynamic can come to feel quite juicy. We might say the equivalent of 'good job' to ourselves in response to our own positive choices and actions, and that's where the internal conversation ends; and spend much of our time getting drawn into the negative conversations with ourselves: *blah, blah, blah, yadda, yadda, yadda* – handing ourselves virtual $100 bills in response to our own negativity.

This, then, is how relationship unfortunately lands and locks in for the vast majority of us. It becomes the basis for how we relate to ourselves and how we relate to others.

We all want close connection and intimacy. We all want to feel the life force of those who are meaningful to us, and to be able to share all the intensity we possess with those people. Even if we are extremely introverted, we find our ways to get plugged in. Children brilliantly and readily read how that is best available, and they act accordingly. They go to negativity because they sense it's their quickest, hottest, most reliable and most profound way to feel closely connected and intimate. And it isn't only children who do this. We all do.

So many of us adults are deeply conditioned to fall into the gravity of putting more energy toward what's going wrong than what's going right. If they are grown-up intense children, as I am, their temptation to get pulled into negativity is strong, because that's where the juice has always been.

The more intense person is strongly drawn to an upside-down energetic message. As he longs for a level of connection to match his intensity, he has difficulty resisting the styles that will reliably draw focus, attention, relationship and energy from the people in his life. This is why a challenging child will break rules and act out even in the face of dire punishment–indeed, why those same punishments can feel a lot like rewards, since they often involve even more intensely charged relationship with important adults. This is why a challenging adult will frequently find herself in the midst of difficulty and conflict despite her best efforts to stay out of trouble, enjoying the drama even as she feels lousy about its consequences.

Just as conventional approaches from educators, parents and psychotherapists can make the intense child's situation worse by inadvertently giving further energy to the problems and issues surrounding negativity, conventional adult therapeutic approaches and relationship advice can often feed a problem-focused view of the world—an approach that, paradoxically, creates fertile ground for depression and anxiety, which in turn creates a multi-billion dollar antidepressant and anti-anxiety medication industry. Why should I give up having issues, problems and negativity when it is so clearly problems that keep people close and coming back?

Neither child nor adult does this consciously. Going into negativity and problems has energetic rewards. We move toward those rewards like moths to flame, especially if we do not find those rewards in more positive places.

Along with this comes a confused and conflicted sense of needing to create problems just to feel alive, seen and acknowledged. The problems still hurt; the damage done to relationships and lives is clear; but that surfeit of intensity keeps driving the bus into the ditch of negativity unless a more positive realm becomes accessible.

# Catching Ourselves
# Being Great

Most of us feel more present and 'alive' when we are faced with problematic thoughts. Our energies are strongly awakened by problems. Unfortunately, we rarely feel we're completely covering ourselves against every potential risk. Awareness of each possible problem might give momentary satisfaction, but it then hatches awareness of more problems. Even financially and professionally successful people are plagued by anxieties and fears about failing in some way. For all but the most highly evolved human beings, greater success brings greater pressure. It rarely reduces our worries, miseries, or doubts; really, it is more likely to amplify them.

Conversely, most of us are low-key when it comes to acknowledging successes or expressing gratitude. Compared to the non-stop, fight-or-flight, wild-and-woolly reactivity that typically accompanies WMDs, focusing on the good does not feel too exciting to most of us. It doesn't really feel like "home."

For our ancestors, constant vigilance against danger was a matter of survival. Our success as a species rested upon our superior ability to imagine what might go wrong in brilliant detail, and on remaining poised to act quickly in response to the first hint of a problem. We wouldn't be here unless they were sufficiently talented at seeing tiny increments of 'wrongness,' which alerted them to possible impending danger.

Fast-forward a few million years. We are still great at seeing tiny increments of what's wrong, but today, we have much less need for this kind of vigilance. In all but the most disadvantaged parts of the world, life is much safer than it once was. The wiring of our brains hasn't caught up to the evolution of our culture. We are still wired to maintain that gift for seeing, microscopically, what is wrong with the picture.

How many worries, miseries and doubts (WMDs) can you conjure up on a moment's notice? I have found that most anyone can find at least a few things wrong with their world, at any moment. I bet most everyone could fill an entire page or an entire conversation with concerns about each issue without missing a beat.

Even when we try to "catch goodness" – which many do in an attempt to create a more positive mindset – we are set up for comparative failure. We tend to set the bar high for noticing desirable qualities like kindness, respect, consideration, helpfulness, and responsibility, barely commenting on these until their demonstration reaches arbitrary high-water marks; but we can wax poetic about disrespect, dishonesty and irresponsibility at the drop of a hat.

We desperately need a way of going from catching goodness to *creating greatness.* This will move us to a more magnificent way of being in the world – a way that many sense is possible, but may have seemed to be beyond their grasp.

Even if you consider yourself to be a relatively positive person, consider the "charge" or level of energy you give to worry, misery and doubt. Is it stronger than the energy you feel around successes? Are you more available, vivid and emotional when something's wrong? When you catch up with friends, what parts of the conversation get the most excited levels of exchange? When you are alone with yourself, which aspects of your life take up more of your inner dialogue? In comparison: how well do we launch the argument for what is already going right? How vivid are our positive comments? What recognitions do we make for what is done well, or even just not done badly?

Most of us get stuck energizing the negative because it's what we learn. It's what we know. The vast and explicit language of what's wrong far exceeds the pale and paltry language of success. We follow our hunger for connection into the rabbit hole of defaulting to negativity, and we often do so without realizing we have a choice in the matter.

The first step toward living your greatness is recognizing how often your mental 'tapes' are playing some version of worry, misery, and doubt; the next step is recognizing that this isn't some broader reality being lived out in your head – it's a choice.

If your life seems full of problems, consider the possibility that at some level, you may be inadvertently invoking and even multiplying the presence of problems in your life by entertaining the alluring 'energy' that attracts us to them in the first place.

# Spin
# Doctor

Notice how often negative thoughts, fears and unfounded judgments run the show. Consider the possibility that we can choose differently. We can doctor the spin toward greatness. We may as well: spin is the way of the world anyway.

When I'm traveling, I sometimes turn on the television in the hotel room to wind down at night. Many times, I've seen late-breaking big news stories that the press jumps to cover. Hotels often have news stations bundled on consecutive channels, and when I scroll through them in succession, I see the very same news covered, with dramatically different spin on every station.

If ten of us witness the same incident, the same is likely true for us as well: we'll have our spin. We might as well own it, and we might as well claim the power of seeing that we can weave greatness into the equation if we so desire. These are our moments, and we can edit them however we like.

By default, you edit your every Now; you may as well do it in a way that enhances happiness, confidence, and joy. Recognizing that spin happens no matter what gives me freedom to spin my story in a new way. I'm the director and producer of the movie that is my life, and I can choose to spin my story in favor of greatness. Even if I don't consciously shape my current reality, it is being shaped by my habitual ways of thinking and reacting to others. If I'm going to spin my story, I may as well be intentional about it.

If you're even occasionally stuck in WMDs, consider the possibility that you are *choosing* to 'spin' the rough footage of your life in a way that amps up the WMD drama. The more we spin our stories to emphasize worries, miseries and doubts, the more we reinforce our commitment to them. The loving universe gives us more of what we are committed to having.

You are the producer and director of the movie that is your life. You can tilt the camera any way you choose to capture any next frame. You can construe each frame any way you wish, and you have the rights to the voice-over. Instead of lugging the baggage of WMDs with you into each consecutive moment, you can choose to embrace those moments in the light of greatness. You can let the now dictate itself to you, or you can be a divinely inspired and creative spin doctor who transforms rough footage into a work of art.

# Taking
## a Toll

The Nurtured Heart Approach uses three 'intentions' to guide the spin described in the last chapter in a positive direction. These intentions can inspire freedom to create that spin with greater magnitude and dimensionality. Here is the first of those three intentions.

A man commuting across the Bay Bridge pulls into the lane of a toll taker who is dancing animatedly to music coming from his boom box. The driver remarks that the toll taker seems to be having a great time, and the toll taker replies: "Yes! I am. I'm having a party. I have the best job in the world—an incredible view, lots of nice people to talk to, fresh air to breathe. I get to listen to my favorite music and I can even practice my dancing while I work."

The driver then looks over at the other tollbooths and comments that the other toll takers don't appear to be having that kind of great time. The toll taker replies, "Oh, those guys in the stand-up coffins? They're no fun."

Adopting a "toll taker" attitude means adopting an intention to see and be in greatness. Before we can do this, we must recognize that we have this choice. I clearly remember when I first realized that I was choosing to be one of the "guys in the stand-up coffins" and resolved to make a shift.

I was at a week-long retreat on Whidbey Island, off the coast of Seattle, Washington. Along with about 200 other attendees, I would meditate first thing in the morning, then walk to a nearby field to stand in a circle—a ritual we all shared before each meal. Each day, I stood in that big circle, scanning person after person. One day, it dawned on me that instead of feeling serene, accepting and grateful, I spent most of my time in that circle in a mental space full of negative judgment – despite the glorious, light-filled meditations I had been in just moments before. *She could lose a few pounds. I don't like the look of that guy. That is a really strange outfit! That person's far too happy...she's got to be a phony.*

What's worse, *it was a silent retreat.* I had not spoken to a single person there, and I did not know any other attendees besides the leader. And I still managed to craft detailed negative judgments of pretty much every other participant I laid eyes on. I can't fathom a better illustration of the way judgments pour out of thin air as a result of a negative default setting.

All of my judgments of the others at this retreat were a figment of a mental software program — let's call it Advance Judgment 1.0 — that caused me to download my experience of new people through this filter of negativity. When I stood in that circle of workshop participants, I was as mired in judgmental thoughts as I had been at any previous time in my life. It took a toll on me.

The tolltaker wasn't high on life because he was beating down all his negative thoughts about his job. He was soaring in the opposite direction without giving negativity any of his energy. He was judgmental of his circumstances, but from a positive vantage point. He was judging in greatness.

# Finding
# Freedom

At their worst, negative judgments cross over into prejudices, stereotypes and biases that have been used to justify some of the worst atrocities that humanity has wrought. Bullying, discrimination, genocide, warfare, unequal treatment based on race, class or color – all can be traced back to judgments that cast one group of people as "less than" or "other."

Even if we have done tremendous work toward being egalitarian and transforming our prejudices, we may all find that we hold subtle – if not blatant – degrees of discrimination. How do we turn around and free ourselves from oppression, stereotyping and bias?

My own exploration has led me to see and accept that the potential for bullying, bias, and terror actually exist within me. Although I have been a victim of bullying and discrimination myself, I know that I am capable of doing all these things to others. If I can judge at the small scale, within, I am certainly capable of doing so at a much larger one, in society.

As I end bullying and bias within me, I discover how to truly listen to and love others without discrimination. As I stay open-hearted and loving, I learn to compost unrefined energies that push me toward judgment and separation into greatness.

Bullying cannot truly end outside of me before I quit bullying myself. When I don't honor my greatness – when I fail to be internally loving, projecting "less-ness" and "otherness" onto myself – I stay in a place where discrimination, bias and negative judgment are possible toward all.

I still have to consciously shift away from negative judgments often. When I manifest subtle and not-so-subtle biases and prejudices in thoughts and actions, I notice and forgive myself. I lovingly embrace those discriminatory tendencies long enough to feel that pain; and then, in resetting, I choose to judge, stereotype, and hold biases that are positive. If judgment is in my DNA, I may as well judge in greatness.

Years after standing in that circle on Whidbey Island, I realized that I could give the part of the brain responsible for judging a new and better job. I could choose to judge in greatness instead of judging negatively. Now, when I meet someone new, I almost always prejudge him or her from this vantage point of greatness. I do the same with myself—in the past, the object of just as many of my harsh negative judgments as anyone else. I've gotten so good at this that I can greatness-judge people I've never met before. If I stay in my heart, I can just as easily go on and on about the greatness of a person I've just met as I can go on about someone I've known for a long time. I indulge my creative side through fantastical, ever-expanding ways of seeing, recognizing and describing greatness. It's always 'there for the making,' available through the ways we choose to construe and spin each moment.

My most dramatic experience of defaulting to greatness in this regard was almost like flicking a switch to turn the lights on. I had just arrived at a long-awaited Gabrielle Roth Five Rhythms workshop. At the time, I knew I was still living out a dichotomy: I was espousing positivity but doing battle with WMDs in my own mind and heart. Fresh on the heels of having taught (of all things) radical appreciation at another retreat center, I stepped into a silent introductory session. This famous dance teacher had us move through the room, connecting silently with other participants through movement. For whatever reason, my first five minutes in that activity were dark ones. I was drawn inexplicably into the vortex of negative judgment, silently weaving baseless narratives about all that was wrong with the others. But this time, I realized what I was doing much sooner. As soon as I caught myself, I wanted to turn the lights on in order to mindfully illuminate the situation differently. And I did turn the lights on, in my own way: by immediately and thoroughly viewing each person in goodness.

I began to use my great skill at judging others to seeing their greatness. It was a much better narrative, and a much happier me came through that process. I wasn't trying to be happy; that was just the effect judging in greatness had on me.

We humans have real talent when it comes to judging. Why throw that talent away when it can be put to such great use?

# The Substitute
# Rabbi

On the day of my mother's memorial, the rabbi who knew her was sick. Another rabbi who didn't know my mother at all was asked to take his place. He had to intuit where the great qualities of this woman lay. Somehow, he did, and beautifully.

In the Champaign School District in Illinois, at one of the middle schools, a new child had arrived at the district well into the school year. He went in for his first morning at the new school. His teacher asked the class for two volunteers, arranging for this young man to be one of them. He asked that the two volunteers stand and then requested that the others in the class call out observations of their greatness. The class was able to give wonderful statements of greatness, even to this new student whom no one really knew. His courage, integrity, caring, thoughtfulness and other qualities of greatness were apparent to the others. A few adults happened to be observing in the room that morning, and there was not a dry eye among them.

A friend told me she was able to do this with a 10-month-old baby. She took the time to watch the baby interacting with her parents and her environment and was able to share a long list of qualities of greatness she clearly saw.

This ability is there for all of us, all of the time. Within moments of meeting someone, we can see, feel and intuit that person's greatness. It's one thing to have someone who knows and loves you reflect greatness back to you; it's almost more precious to have a brave soul meet you for the first time and see through to who you really are, in your magnificence and splendor, and to tell you what he or she sees.

# Resistance
## is Futile

The ability to give greatness recognitions is something worth cultivating. It brings joy equivalent to – perhaps greater than – receiving them. And in truth, the ability to *receive* acknowledgments of greatness without deflecting or denying them tests a person to the core, and also requires dedicated practice. I see anyone able to drink in an intense greatness recognition, and to allow it to be as nourishing as it can be, as highly accomplished. It reflects upon the 'work' they have done to be able to resonate at that level of greatness. If I am determined to tell that person of their greatness, no amount of resistance will dissuade me. And believe me – I've seen a lot of people resist this as though it were a threat to their very being. It can feel that way to be held in greatness when we are strongly attached to and defined by negativity.

Any resistance from the recipient makes me want to turn up the dial to get through to them, to enable them to hear and breathe in the truth of what's being reflected: "I can tell my words fell a little flat, and that it was hard for you to hear that I saw your courage and great intention in the situation you were telling me about. Here's why I said that. It's so easy to turn away in a situation like the one you faced. And you were so kind and thoughtful and honest. That took guts and determination. Those are great qualities I see in you."

If they continue to resist, I persist in turning up the dial: saying what I see with more heart, more evidence, more clarity, more precision and more resolve. Ultimately, they don't stand a chance! If I were relentlessly criticizing the person in question, this might sound cruel, but remember that what I'm driving home is the person's greatness. This is true modern warriorship.

I trust that the recipient, then, is ultimately the winner when I am victorious in my efforts to thoroughly recognize them in greatness. Resistance is indeed futile. A world where people do this for each other is the world I want to live in. How about you?

# Godness vs.
# Greatness

*A Hindu man saw a scorpion floundering around in the water. He decided to save it by stretching out his hands, but the scorpion stung him. The man still tried to get the scorpion out of the water, but the scorpion stung him again. A man nearby told him to stop saving the scorpion that kept stinging him, but the Hindu man said, "It is the nature of the scorpion to sting. It is my nature to love. Why should I give up my nature to love just because it is the nature of the scorpion to sting?"*

I don't want be good for the sake of being good. I don't want to be good for political reasons or societal reasons. I don't want to be good for religious reasons, philosophical reasons or any other reason. What I want is to internally celebrate and generate greatness. I want that greatness to emanate from me as an unstoppable force from within, like a bubbling brook that simply flows all day, every day, because that is its nature. And if I get stung in the process of sending that greatness out into the world and building it in myself, so be it. The Hindu man in the story knows his nature is loving; I know that my nature is greatness.

I know our true nature is greatness. This universal truth lies beneath all of what we think is currently our true nature.

Good people follow the rules, we think, and bad people break them. But I don't want to follow the rules because of some idea that following the rules makes me a good person. Rule-following is far from a guarantee of goodness, safety, success or enlightenment. You can get your eight hours of sleep and be outplayed or outperformed by the person who stays up half the night. The person using bad language or poor manners or poor technique can out-sell you or out-shine you. You can eat by the rules and be overweight and then resent people who eat everything and don't exercise and still look like a million bucks. It's easy to wind up resenting people who don't play by the rules and are clearly having more fun and enjoying greater success. "Foul!" we call when following the rules doesn't lead us to happily-ever-after. "Unfair!" We can play by all the rules of "good" and still have our juiciest internal relationship with negative thoughts.

The problem with good is that it's tethered forever to bad. A news station can rededicate itself over and over to sharing good news, but at the end of the day, bad news is what sells. When disaster hits, every station gives way to the unfolding story. They all grant it endless airtime because they know they risk losing viewers to other stations who give it more coverage. They will never give good news more than a brief spot and a limited perspective, whereas negative news will get dissected every which way, ten times over.

Normally, the energy we give to celebrating the good is nowhere near the energy, presence and relationship we pour out so readily and frequently when things are bad. Bad, then, easily and inadvertently becomes the cultural 'password' to feeling alive by way of that much juicier conversation, which insidiously seeps into the consciousness of both individuals and the collective. As this becomes our personal default and set point, we barely realize the extent to which it has gained the all-access backstage pass to our minds. Worse, we wind up magnetically attracting more negativity, because the loving universe recognizes how alive and energized we are around these WMDs. It 'interprets' this to mean that we love negativity. The loving universe honors the truth of our devoted energy and the focus of our minds and hearts, and will give each of us more of what we love.

What people create, day to day, reflects what they are truly committed to. You can say you want to be more "good," but as long as you continue to hang out in that dichotomy, bad comes along for the ride, and you're likely to keep giving it your most 'alive' energy. We vote with our energy and the way we weave that energy into actions, thoughts, emotions and relationship. You can say you love the positive all day long, but if your energy to the negative is what really captures you – if that is what you give *YOU* to - then that's what you really love.

We must exit that realm entirely. Beyond good and bad lies greatness. Your greatness-nature is yours, now, and will always be – even if you get stung sometimes. Greatness is the common denominator, the foundation of all that is. It is its own reward.

> *Out beyond ideas of wrongdoing*
> *and rightdoing there is a field.*
> *I'll meet you there.*
> *When the soul lies down in that grass*
> *the world is too full to talk about.*
>
> - Rumi

*Good* is a set-up that draws us again and again into bad. Greatness is the field where souls can meet. It is the escape valve that transcends and resets the internal GPS. It realigns the map to deliver us to endless next iterations in the journey to who we really are. Truth is, that location, that longitude and latitude of you in greatness is there, whether you choose to enter that slipstream or not. You cannot escape breathing and you cannot escape greatness. Breathing deeper is always possible, and is almost always sweet; so, too, is purposefully entering into and collaborating with greatness. Going deeper into greatness is more accessible than most people know, and there is no bottom to its depths.

If this mindset challenges you – if you can't quite yet gauge greatness as relating to you – here is another perspective. In my own experience, when something is not-great, it conjures up a picture of the sweetness of how great GREAT is.

Let's say your child is choosing to play at the computer at the moment, which gives you a precious break for some reading. How *not-great* would it be right now if your child was whining to you for something or being argumentative, rude or disrespectful? It would be *very* not-great, wouldn't it? Maybe even *very, very* not-great?

If you have a child, has he or she ever been rude, whiny, disrespectful or argumentative? Remembering that the child is capable of this helps you see the preciousness of moments when he or she isn't doing any of those things.

Right at this moment, your child is *being* the greatness of *not being* rude and *not being* disrespectful, along with *not being* argumentative and *not being* whiny. That alone shows the child's thoughtfulness, compassion, caring, wisdom, self-control, and personal power. And there's so much more. These are all qualities of greatness, aren't they?

We can easily transpose this barometer to gauging *your* greatness at the moment. It is always there for the taking. What are you *not* doing right now that could be annoying, challenging or downright treacherous? Those are all victories, and all point back to aspects of your greatness.

My faith is in greatness. My experience is that if I can achieve and claim one more micron of greater greatness – if I can climb a little further up the mountain of greatness, just around one more bend – the rippling of greatness out into the world and into my life is tremendous. Stresses, issues, and problems that exist at my current level of greatness become non-issues at some next, greater level.

When I shared this with someone, her response was, "If you take one step toward God, God will take ten toward you." This has been exactly my experience in my study and expression of greatness. If you take one step toward your greatness or the greatness of others, then greatness will step forward to meet you. And like many great software programs, greatness comes bundled with extras and surprises that upgrade everything: from the way you feel inside to the way you look at things, to the way others look at you and up to you.

# Great
# Addictions

From very early on, I noticed that creating chaos, havoc and drama got me the strongest forms of relationship and energy from others and from myself – a far stronger hit than any success I could manage. A later addiction to mind-altering substances seemed like a natural evolution. In the 1980s, I fell into a period of experimenting with alcohol, marijuana, cocaine and more. Although I escaped without any visible scars, I did the addiction thing full-tilt. I did a lot of whatever I was doing, often risking getting arrested or killed or killing myself with an overdose.

Between descents into this place, I would enter a passionate aftermath where I would pledge to take better care of myself. I didn't use. I ate well and got my life back on track. But I lacked the inner wealth to sustain that state of stability. Whether I was up or down, I was still essentially in relationship with these same issues, bumping into different walls of the same house.

Most people look at addiction as a two-sided coin: the bad part (when you're using) and the good part (when you're not). But the entire cycle of addiction and recovery is a kind of full-frontal nudity with your misery, a perpetuation of an internal dialogue that feeds the fire of problems with an intensity that can seem irresistible. Even in the midst of my healthy periods, I was still having the same internal conversation with myself. The theme was always the same: *problems*. At the time, I had no idea of how to escape this trap. I was craving intense relationship, which turned me into a magnet for situations where I could keep the WMDs rolling. The loving universe saw that I had the juiciest relationship with myself when I pushed my limits or when I was hanging out in a risky situation and then subsequently kicked my own butt about how bad that was. The loving universe then, lovingly, handed me more opportunity for the same. I did not have the wherewithal to say anything but yes. Energetically, I was demonstrating that I loved misery. I was misery; so I attracted more misery. I thought I was getting high, but in truth, I was getting misery. And the more I ran *from* misery, the more I ran right into...*more* misery.

The addict is seeking happiness. Any commercial or advertisement for alcoholic drinks will depict the quite pleasurable, usually social, side of having a drink or two. When you have a drink at a bar, sometimes you might end up feeling pleasantly giddy and meeting someone with whom you have a nice time. Then you come down, and you don't feel quite so good, and you stop meeting sexy strangers, and you think: *Hmmm, maybe what I need to do is go back to that bar for another drink.* And you have that drink, but you don't feel as good as you remember feeling last time. No sexy stranger to chat with tonight, either. So, in search of some remnant of that past happiness, you have another drink. Soon you wind up exposed to all kinds of misery – not the happiness with which you had originally associated those initial drinks on that night when it all worked out. In the aftermath, you feel lousy. You have that conversation with yourself again...and before you know it, you're off to the bar for another handful of drinks.

How do we stop loving misery? There's so much energy in that tumble from grace that follows any form of barreling down problematic roads. The energy of the self-talk and the energy of the negative situations that transpire in relation to addictions is the perpetuating power that keeps this whole pattern spinning.

To quit for good, you have to choose to love something more than your addiction. You refuse to enter into those conversations that are essentially a seductive striptease for misery. Even if you screw something up, you feel it deeply and as briefly as possible. Despite temptation to give it lots of conversation, you opt out. Shift gears in a flash, even when the siren song of misery is calling your name.

I'm not going to pretend I have no fear or dread. But when those feelings arise, I feel them deeply, efficiently and swiftly, then tap into that energy of worry and put it to work in a better direction in accordance with my inner compass. From that deep well of magnetism, I magnetize a force that ultimately brings me to a more enlightened sense of who I really am. This is what I'm addicted to now: climbing that trajectory of greatness.

This exploration of what's possible in greatness has also manifested many new friendships that are more alive, upbeat, and energetically congruent. The conversation is fun, alive, enhancing, and supportive, and the banter is at no one's expense. Most of the times the drink of choice is water, and that suits me fine.

# No Matter
# What

A friend of mine fell 28 feet from a roof and badly injured his face and jaw. After moving through a long, arduous recovery, he told me that when he awakened in the hospital, he was immediately grateful to be alive. Knowing how far he'd fallen, he felt blessed that he could even feel his body.

My friend shared that when he'd awoken to consciousness, his mouth was swollen shut. He remembered his doctors saying that when the swelling receded in the days that followed, they would begin reconstruction of his jaw and face, and that they would try to accomplish as much of the reconstructive surgery as they could through his mouth, but most likely would have to do a fair amount of work through his eye sockets or even by making an incision at his hairline and peeling back the skin of his face. Hearing this, I was glad to be sitting down, because if I had been standing, my knees would have buckled.

"That must have sounded absolutely horrifying!" I said.

My friend told me he hadn't felt that way. What he remembered was feeling like everything was going to be okay. He could remember sending positive thoughts to his doctor and feeling instantly grateful to be blessed with the best medical team he could've hoped for. He was glad that his doctors would be able to accomplish most of what was necessary through easier, less intrusive routes.

"There's always a hidden lesson," he told me, "so why not feel blessed knowing that you are in the midst of it? You eventually have to deal with everything, so why not have a positive attitude from the very first moments of anything and everything? Why not be in gratitude no matter what?" I was in awe of his exalted attitude of gratitude, and told him so. I asked him what had shaped his amazing way of looking at life.

"When I was a teenager, I had an older friend who was stuck in a wheelchair. He had some kind of progressive degenerative disease," he told me. "We would play chess together. I remember asking him what he would want if he could have three wishes. And his wishes were: 'One: to walk. Two, to walk. And three, to walk.'" He took a deep breath, remembering that moment. "I said to myself, wow – *I'm already living out this person's three wishes.*" From that point, his default setting clicked into inspired gratitude.

From that point forward, my friend's default was to be grateful *no matter what;* to find a positive slant on every situation; and to see that since he would have to deal with everything eventually, *no matter what,* he might as well climb into that great attitude immediately...*no matter what.*

Since then, every time I've thought of my friend, I want to honor the greatness that he lives and loves. Every time I think of his astounding attitude—his beauty, poise, grace, verve, stamina, power, presence, compassion, earnestness, and heart—and his friend ("To walk. To walk. To walk")—I'm rendered speechless again, stilled in a moment full of greatness.

I commit to seeing greatness in myself and others, *no matter what.*

Let's walk in greatness with all we already have, *no matter what.*

# Quit Praying
## for Peace

Prayers for peace often occur in response to news of what we don't want: a stabbing, a riot, genocide, a terrorist act, a school shooting. When I pray or hope under these circumstances, I am acting under the belief that my talisman of prayer for peace can somehow fight, in the ether, the energy of that unwanted thing. But in innocently praying for peace in response to a hatred of war, or in hoping for prosperity in response to a fear of poverty, I inadvertently give my heartfelt personal energy, perhaps the most powerful gift I possess, to what I *don't* want. I give the *gift of me* to what I *don't* want. I'm rowing hard, with plenty of heart…in the wrong direction.

What if, instead of praying or hoping for peace, I say, "I am peace" or "We are peace?" Can I find instances in my life where I can acknowledge peace in myself and in those with whom I interact? Could it be that I am *being peace* when I choose to get along with anyone? What if, any time I am not being violent, I am choosing peace, and I can choose to acknowledge that as an expression of my greatness?

Even those who struggle with urges to harm others or themselves, but do not act on them, are embodying peace. Peace is actually the predominant energy of most people in most places at most times. It is the predominant energy of all beings on the planet. The miracle we want may be the miracle already in existence: of seven billion people on the planet, perhaps *only a million* or so are being violent at any given time. Imagine if that number were two million or ten million. How *not* great would that be? It stands to energetic reason that we can be grateful for the peace that already exists.

We all know someone who we've experienced as not being honest, not using integrity, not being respectful, or not being responsible. It's pretty evident in those instances how *not* great these situations are.

Qualities like respect, responsibility, integrity, honesty and more are truly qualities of greatness. Seeing what negative circumstances *aren't* happening that *could* be happening is one way of shedding light on the expression of these qualities. But here is another inference 'non-greatness' highlights for me: even a *shred* of evidence of any quality of greatness is indeed proof that greatness is there.

Both of these perspectives – allowing non-greatness to point the way to greatness, and allowing even the smallest molecule of greatness to demonstrate that much more is available – are ways of diving into what greatness is and impelling ourselves and others to recognize it. We are so willing to notice and comment on not-greatness. Can we compel ourselves to comment in appreciation of the actual greatness that is companion to virtually any unfolding moment?

The overwhelming majority of people on this earth are upholding peace – "being" peace – right now. Peacemaking and peacekeeping require kindness, thoughtfulness, consideration, love, and appreciation. Most of the humans on the planet right now are living out these great qualities, either actively or passively. This is the miracle I want to energize further. I don't want to inadvertently give even an ounce of my energy to the negativity of non-peace.

Peace is happening all the time. The same goes for other positive things for which I might hope and pray: love, prosperity, beauty, and harmony. If there is something I want more of, instead of butting heads with and giving my precious energy to its opposite, I can notice and acknowledge its presence all around me in this moment.

As a child, I often heard adults using the expression "save your soul." At the time, I didn't give it much thought; but since I began to teach the Nurtured Heart Approach, this expression has taken on a much deeper meaning for me.

Your life force, your being, your soul is the supreme gift you can give to anyone or any thing. This approach and this practice are about choosing to save your soul for all that is great, and to give generously to all we can see pointing in that direction.

We so generously project greatness onto those who become our heroes in sports, and into matters of the heart or matters of social justice, but we tend to be so very frugal in giving this gift to ourselves, to others close at hand, or to everyday joys and victories. Giving appreciation of greatness *everywhere, no matter what,* reserves the generosity of our spirits for what we truly want.

# Better
# Broadband

I want a dedicated, high-capacity, always-online, lightning-fast connection to the Internet...and I want the same kind of connection to my own greatness.

More and more of us are seeking some way to connect with an energy beyond the humdrum grind of daily life. We want a connection to sacred mystery, spirit and greatness. Some lucky ones fall into it by accident, getting just a fleeting, delicious taste before losing hold of it again. Few of us have reliable roadmaps to lead us there over and over. Even if we have moments of insight or enlightenment, most of us lack concrete action steps to get back on the horse after we've fallen off. Sometimes we don't catch ourselves back in the world of WMDs (worry, misery, doubt) until we've been there for days, weeks, months or even years. Life can easily sweep us into the vortex of not remembering and feeling disconnected.

If you were knocked offline while using your computer, you'd be immediately aware of this. You'd do whatever was necessary – call tech support, reboot, jiggle wires – to get back online. For most of us, a few days offline at the computer would be unthinkable, let alone a few months. But we can easily fall offline from greatness for much longer without even realizing it. Once offline, it can be a long journey (without much tech support) back to a place of connection to what really matters.

Since creating my new "default setting" of being online to greatness, I much more readily notice when I fall offline. In effect, I've created that as a 'dedicated line!' I've learned to instantly notice when I'm offline to my greatness and I've inherently learned how to get back to where I belong.

Begin to notice when you're offline from greatness. Get to know the part of yourself that is capable of noticing it – your inner tech support guru. Let this disconnection create urgency as real as the urgency you experience when you can't connect to the Internet. Allow it to activate the part of yourself that doesn't want to muck around in WMDs when so much greatness is available.

# Baby
# Stepping

Imagine a baby getting ready to take her first steps.

It's hard not to get truly excited about even the prospect of a first step. Even our anticipated responses cannot come close to the feelings that arise in response to even the first efforts a baby makes to stand. Even when the 'almost' step happens, joy often simply erupts—even when we try to maintain some semblance of dignified poise.

Imagine this baby doing that thing babies do when they're about to lurch into those first upright strides: holding on to something, rocking, huffing and making adorable baby sounds, and then—surprise!...one step, and then another!

And inevitably...then, she's down. Plop! Right on her rear.

What's your reaction? What's the first thing you say?

Do you say, "That was pretty good, but your form could have been improved on!"

Do you say, "Two steps? All right, but now, let's see you take ten."

Of course not! If you're someone who can muster actual words in the face of this kind of intense cuteness, you're more likely to say something like, "Oh my goodness! You did it! You took your first steps!"

"Yay! Amazing! Wonderful!"

...or perhaps, you are one of those people who can do nothing but make squeaky, squealing, whooping sounds under such circumstances. At any rate, there's something about the sight of a baby taking its first steps that blows our hearts right open. Any expression that comes through us in the moment of connecting with that baby is coming straight from the source of what's great; because, deep down, we truly see it as great.

And from that point forward, we celebrate every increment of that baby's progress toward walking. There's no stress, no hurry, no pressure, but when the baby moves in that developmental direction, positive acknowledgements pour out of all but the most resistant adults. We wouldn't think to be critical or to point out lack or shortcoming. Even if that baby was developmentally different and walked late, or perhaps might never walk at all, the adults charged with her care would find ways to connect with and encourage her movement toward greater functionality and independence.

If we have the required awareness and language, we are likely to seed the steps before they even begin. We might applaud with awe and appreciation the sense that this baby is watching a sibling walk and looking like the possibility of doing the same thing is beginning to dawn on him. We might admiringly enjoy how she exercises her legs and arms in the most rudimentary ways—a prelude to pulling herself off of the ground. Our hearts tell the story of our love of this child and her budding accomplishments.

Unfortunately, we tend to lose that instinctive sense of highly responsive delight as our children leave baby-hood. Our expectations become harder and harder to meet. Before we know it, we might be sitting that child down – that child who was once that delightful baby, whose every coo and wiggle made our hearts spring open and our voices sing out impromptu acknowledgements – and giving her a lecture about how her behavior or her grades or her life choices could stand improvement.

To internalize this second "intention" of the Nurtured Heart Approach, hold in your awareness the image of that baby taking its first steps. Try to recall how that baby can really do no wrong. There are no strict expectations, just joy and awe in the moment. There is no bar held high; just a highly attentive and heart-open state where every tiny increment in the right direction is something to recognize, appreciate, acknowledge and celebrate. Starting with this heart-full, heart-open awareness guarantees success. Creating success is an art, an intention and a mindset—

really, a *heart-set*—that opens up opportunities for gratitude and greatness in place of criticism, dissatisfaction and frustration.

Let's be clear: that baby is going to walk better and better whether we sing out in excited acknowledgement and wonder or criticize and give pep talks ("Come on, baby, you took one step, and I just KNOW your first marathon is right around the corner, so let's see some effort!"). It's just the great nature of the human being. She will toddle, trip, and fall, and eventually, most likely, she'll move from wobbly walk, to confident stride, to swift run. Even if we try to stop her, success is inevitable, barring a disability that impacts this process.

Melissa, my coauthor, had one child who walked very early, at eight and a half months. One doctor encouraged her to try to slow the process down, as if the child didn't intrinsically know, with every fiber of her being, that it was time for her to walk. Suffice it to say that Melissa had zero success with that endeavor. Her daughter's great determination won out, and she was running within the month. She is now an accomplished dancer who loves every minute of gliding through her universe.

Why not create a situation where success is the primary possibility; offer energized gratitude for that success; and let the energy of that greatness and momentum feed the next levels of success? Who could this possibly hurt?

When I try to teach parents the methodology of the Nurtured Heart Approach, and I tell them the method involves noticing and acknowledging how the child is moving in the right direction as well as appreciating what isn't going wrong, I am occasionally met with an incredulous look. When battle-weary from parenting a difficult child, adults at first cannot always envision themselves able to find successes to acknowledge.

But if they can see the glorious spirit of that baby beyond even the markers of those first steps to the often untapped realm of exploration *on the way* to those steps, that exploration itself comes to captivate, inspire and thrill them. They begin to feel into the notion that success is not an un-scalable mountain or a bar held high. It's a mindset of fostering the success that already exists in the sprout that reveals itself well before any expectation of harvest. As we acknowledge the beauty of that first inkling of energy in the desired direction, we become a vital part of *creating successes that might not otherwise exist*. We are harvesting a vision of things to come.

Use this "Baby Steps" intention to create successes that you would otherwise not have seen or expressed. Find ways to see and acknowledge the smallest positive choices in others and in yourself. See the miraculous in the shift from sitting to crawling, and then from crawling to pulling up to standing on every object in sight: that inexorable drive to expand and explore coming alive in every cell of that baby's body. See the tiny shifts in weight as the baby dares to let go of the object he's leaning against. See the toes curling, the brow knitted in effort, and those first moments of balancing; see the plopping down and trying again and again. Every moment, every step is its own miracle.

The baby doesn't do this consciously or intentionally. It's just his nature to be great. Every movement and evolution is an expression of that greatness, and it's completely unfettered by ego or fear. Failure is impossible. Begin to see the baby steps happening all around you. Look with fresh eyes at the freshness of everything you and others do in your daily life. Celebrate it. Anoint it with appreciation of its greatness. This is way beyond "catching yourself being good"—we are renewing to "creating being great."

# Greatness
# Whisperer

Right now, you're reading a book that you think might help you improve yourself and your life. Here's what I know about you in this moment, based on that choice:

- You are determined to be your best self.

- You care deeply about how you conduct yourself and how you impact others.

If these things were not true, you would not be reading these words right now.

We could further unwrap the truth of that greatness: Your desire to express all these qualities reveals your compassionate and loving nature as well as your commitment to living a passionate, purposeful life.

If I were working with you to help you apply the Baby Steps intention, I might do a few minutes of 'greatness whispering' to unwrap this further. With ease, I'd be able to express to you even more greatness.

For instance: having a compassionate and loving nature requires you to be daring enough to be in your heart. Not everyone dares this. It is indeed a great quality to care deeply; to feel deeply; and to be discerning and refined enough to think in compassionate and loving ways. It is greatly courageous to choose, again and again, to stay on the side of compassion. Making the hard choices required to do so shows the wealth of your spirit and your willingness to stand in your power.

Let's go deeper. Having a commitment to a purposeful life means that you want to have a positive impact on the world and others. This reveals other qualities of your greatness. It shows that you have a vision beyond any self-serving lifestyle. You care about the world and the feelings and well-being of others. This alone conveys that you are thoughtful and considerate and that you want to see what is best in people. These are incontrovertible reflections of your loving and caring nature, discipline, wisdom, and good judgment.

I hope you see that so much greatness already is within you, and that much more can be cultivated by bringing it into expression. I hope you can feel the truth of this – and that this truth hasn't ruined your day. And, finally, I hope that if I can see this in you, and if you can begin to see it in yourself, you can also see this in others.

# Molecules
# to Miracles

One Monday, you spill coffee on your shirt while driving to work, then arrive late for your 9:00 meeting. As soon as you get there, you realize you've left your presentation materials at home.

Your 'default settings' might bring you to curse yourself out or blame others. "If I hadn't gotten up so late...If I were better organized...If it weren't for that barista who didn't put the lid on all the way...if that guy on the freeway had been driving in the slow lane where he belonged...if my husband had helped more getting the kids out the door to school..." you might have thought or said. Then, you might have spent a good part of the day telling and retelling stories about who was at fault and what could have been done differently.

What if you had said to yourself, in those first moments after calming down from the mayhem of your commute, "I spilled hot coffee on myself while driving, and I didn't lose my cool. I kept driving safely despite my frustration. I managed to laugh at the chaos at breakfast this morning with the kids even though I was rushed and stressed. I remembered to say 'I love you' to my spouse before leaving, and that shows I value my marriage and that I'm serious about expressing my love even when I'm annoyed!"

Have you ever seen someone not handle impulses well? Have you ever seen someone *not engage* their wisdom and self-control? How *not* great is that? When even modest amounts of impulse control and wisdom show up in yourself or others, be thankful, and express your gratitude.

Most people in our society don't know how to dissect scenarios and human interactions in a way that reveals the greatness underlying those interactions. They don't know how to tease any given circumstance into its component parts of greatness – what is sitting there, waiting to be seen, in terms of a child's or adult's actions, thoughts and expressions.

A small expression is worth savoring. Even a hair's-breadth of recognition is a valuable beginning of an energizing pattern. Acknowledging something as great sets it into a trajectory toward expanding greatness; however, it's the initial launch of energy towards what you deem to be great that plants the seed. Without that initiative, that first shift, no growth can get underway. A third intention helps lend deeper dimension to this direction.

As a child, I observed that any poor choices I made – really, almost anything "less" or flawed or problematic – were summarily put under a microscope, cross-examined, and blown out of proportion with reactions, sermons and lectures. I affectionately think back on this as the adults having made "mountains out of molehills." My parents or teachers were skilled at this, but at times, it seemed that every adult in our zip code was engaged in a secret competition: who could make the biggest mountain out of the smallest molehill?

Then, years later, it dawned on me that this very skillset, so often taken down a negative road, reflected a highly creative ability – even an artistic talent – that could be activated from a diametrically opposed frame of reference. One could *create miracles from molecules.* One could take a warrior stance of 'hijacking' the smallest bits and pieces of greatness observable, providing recognition and appreciation for them. Not past, not future: Just the truth of the moment.

What qualities of greatness must you have in order to drive safely despite pain and frustration created by a coffee spill? How about the greatness of focus; the greatness of good reflexes; the greatness of calmness and clarity? Your ability to laugh at breakfast table chaos points to the greatness of having a sense of humor, a balanced point of view, and a high valuation of your relationship with your children. It demonstrates resiliency and determination to mine joy, even when life is challenging.

And then, you can take it even further by seeing greatness in the choices you *didn't* make. Feeling the impulse to do something wrong isn't a crime. When that impulse is resisted, it's a victory. Who hasn't had the feeling of wanting to break something? As long as you haven't actually done the breaking, you've made a great decision not to be destructive.

On a tough morning drive, you didn't lapse into road rage; instead, you exercised wisdom, self-control and good judgment. You didn't burst into tears when you realized you'd left your materials at home; instead, you found a way to give your presentation without the handouts you prepared. That's your greatness of ingenuity shining through.

The standard response of giving energy to negativity inadvertently deepens our impression that unwanted behaviors are highly meaningful. We keep returning to those behaviors to get energetic 'liftoff,' especially as long as little to no energy moves in response to *desired* behaviors. Holding an intention of creating successes by making miracles from molecules makes more visible the river of greatness that runs through every moment. Once you catch a glimpse of it, you learn to look in its direction as a matter of habit.

# On Inner
# Wealth

When I make a concerted effort to stand in greatness, more and more greatness comes my way. And each pearl of greatness I burnish in myself and see in others contributes to the cause of what I call *inner wealth.*

Inner wealth is a currency that accrues within us as we commit to seeing and expanding greatness. It is a progressive deepening into seeing the beauty of a purposeful life; of knowing who we are in relation to the greatness of all that includes each and every one of us. In coming to "know who we are," we accrue a growing sense of the unique characteristics that are streams contributing to our rivers of generative prowess: our idiosyncratic qualities of wisdom, kindness, magnetism, beauty, compassion, and honesty. As these qualities inevitably flow into the ocean of our being, we not only come to know who we are in progressively profound ways, but we progress in our ability to love the distinctive delivery system of this constellation of greatness: ourselves! Inner wealth eclipses self-esteem. It envelops and expands upon it.

The more we come to appreciate the uncommon, special greatness of our selves, the more we can appreciate the nuanced greatness of others. With inner wealth, we come to see others' uniqueness instead of stereotyping and categorizing. Negative judgments transform to judgments pertaining to greatness. Giving becomes more comfortable as we experience greatness as a vast place of inner abundance. We find less separation of beings at the soul level.

As inner wealth grows, we become increasingly attuned to our own gratitude and intuition, like a musical instrument attuned to a higher-frequency vibration. The universe then collaborates at that exact frequency, dialing it in like a radio station: "Okay, if you're going to be great, I'll support you in that."

Greatness is inherent in all of us; it needs only to be awakened. We are all born into greatness, but almost all of us forget this as we are exposed to the gravity of the world. Recognitions of greatness help us remember what is already there. They build inner wealth. Through inner wealth, we can move beyond the current conceptualization of wealth in terms of haves versus the have-nots, or of the one percent versus the 99 percent. In the realm of Inner Wealth, we can all be billionaires.

This is not a skill that comes naturally to most of us; if we are accustomed to living as though the glass were half empty instead of half full, we may need some specific guidance or techniques for spotting and acknowledging greatness in vivid detail. The second section of this book contains all you will need toward that end.

Really, though, this goes beyond seeing the glass as half full or half empty. Even if barely a drop remains in the glass, we can choose to appreciate and feel gratitude for that one shimmering drop. We can even see beauty in any hint of what we imagine *might* have been in the glass! In choosing to weave this kind of narrative, we purposefully make the most of every opportunity to see and expand greatness.

Every being has signed up for greatness. Said another way: greatness is inherently in every person's hardware. The problem is that most of us have gotten many endless, subtle contradictions along the way – downloads of software that oppose greatness. As soon as we receive the new, enhanced software and hit a threshold of inner wealth, most of us remember who we really are. We grow in confidence; we become increasingly inspired. As we gain altitude, we find that we can fly.

# Video Game
# Theory

When I was counseling families with intense, difficult children, parents would often mention that this child, who could not sit still in a classroom for five minutes without causing a disruption, was able to sit in front of video or computer games for hours straight. Intense children could play these games with singular focus and determination. Their motivation to hit level after level after level of mastery and accomplishment seemed stronger than that of less intense children. "Why can't my child be this way about school work, chores, or good behavior?" these parents would ask.

Research shows that people of all ages with ADHD, anxiety or depression are at greater risk for developing an addiction to video games. I would maintain that intense adults get hooked on these stimulating environments for the same reasons as intense children.

What might those reasons be? Video games offer:

1. *Immediate and reliable recognition of success.* A profound level of energy transpires when players move in the right direction through skilled actions and choices. Players are confronted with their success through points scored or through sounds and visual effects. The player gets big hits of energy that are congruent with successful choices.

2. *Consistent expectations and rules, with immediate accountability when lines are crossed or wrong moves are made.* When the player makes a mistake, there is simply a momentary loss of the energy given by the game, marked by a very short loss of connection – a "reset."

3. *An immediate default setting back to success.* Within moments of a game-ending or penalty-exacting choice, the player

can get right back into the game, starting completely fresh. The player has absolute freedom to break the rules of the game; when he or she does, the game gives that player what amounts to a simple reset.

The game doesn't offer lectures about how the player could have avoided this consequence. Nor does it give warnings or threats when players seem about to break a rule. The consequences may seem drastic and punitive (heads rolling, bombs bursting) – but who's back in the game in a second or two, more determined than ever to *not* break the game's rules, and to earn more points in this new round?

The game gives an energetic illusion of a consequence, then moves the player back into the game. In a way, the game's default setting is to greatness. The video game consequence is really a built-in 'kiss' of forgiveness that leads straight into the next moment of success. Players receive a steady flow of positive feedback and unlimited "do-overs," leading inexorably toward motivated mastery and accomplishment: greatness.

The way to create this irresistible video game dynamic for yourself is through constant recognition of yourself for even small increments of success, creating a steady flow of positive feedback. Confront yourself with the energy of appreciation (game-in/game-on); refuse to energize the negative (more on this later); and give yourself a brief reset when something goes awry (game out/game off). Consider any failure to be a brief pause on your way to the next success.

# The Energy-Challenged
# Adult

When I look at an intense child, it is easy for me to see the beauty of that intensity even when it is being expressed in strongly negative behaviors. Even with that first glance, I can see how that same life force can be re-routed positively to serve the child and the world. My mother's intensity was another story.

She died in 2008, finally letting go at the age of 96. While she was alive, I was stuck in a short view of her as someone whose life was hampered by a staggering degree of worry, fear, doubt and misery. It took her death to wake me up to the fact that her enormous intensity was attached to an enormous wealth of life force that was largely untapped and was rarely directed into positive endeavors. In all her life, she never had anyone hold her in greatness. How terribly sad.

Only after her death did I come to recognize that her intensity, which usually manifested as overwhelming anxiety, came from a deep well of caring. She loved so deeply that she could hardly stand it or contain it, much less express it. I got that this intensity that came out of her sideways as fear and doubt was really a tenacity and determination that could move mountains. I got that her intense judgment of others was actually a greatness of integrity. She wanted things to be fair and equitable. She wanted what was right and fair for her family and for others she cared about.

Her life, to me, seemed lived in lockstep with WMDs. But after her death, I was able to see how her great life force had been kept hidden from view. Her positive qualities, woven into the fabric of worry, misery and doubt, had a greatness I had not been able to recognize before.

Might outward recognition of her qualities of greatness have relieved her of the burden of her anxiety and fears? How might her awakening to her greatness have opened life to her, enabling her to put these qualities to work in positive ways? I'll never know. It's fun to imagine how this might have transformed her.

It was exciting to take a fresh look at my mother's life and to see her greatness for the very first time. Seeing this inspired me to ramp up my determined efforts to do this with others before it's too late.

I would like to think that as we pass out of this life, we might be greeted by a vivid, ecstatic lightning bolt that illuminates the truth of greatness in and around us. In those final moments, I like to think that we are met with a vision of who we are that we couldn't otherwise see – aspects that are beckoning to be awakened.

I don't want to wait until someone's memorial service to speak to his or her greatness. Memorials and funerals are more socially acceptable times to speak of this subject; otherwise, it tends to be handled awkwardly or not handled at all. Even if a soul could, somehow, hear honoring words from beyond the grave, I'd dread thinking it was the first time it ever heard about its greatness.

I've used the energy of my grief about my mother's journey to dedicate myself to more proactively growing greatness in myself and in others. We can all undergo the process of dying into greatness while we are still alive.

# The Alchemy
## of Emotion

Consider a baby. One moment she's screaming inconsolably. The next, she's laughing. As she grows, she loses this ability to let her emotions ride through her like the log flume at the amusement park. This is a necessary evolution. Adults don't ordinarily let loose a torrent of tears or a joyful outburst just anywhere. Eruptions of pure feeling from a person over the age of four tend to make other people uncomfortable.

In modern life, we've learned to hide and resist feelings a little too well. Many of the stresses modern adults encounter have to do with an inability to recognize, experience and move through more challenging feeling states. Emotional intelligence—the ability to feel and manage the full spectrum of human emotions—isn't taught in most schools or in most households. Few of us were lucky enough to have it modeled by our parents or other important adults when we were children; most require guidance – a curriculum of some kind, like the Nurtured Heart Approach – to adequately impart it to our children.

Human beings experience emotion in our bodies. We feel anger in the guts, joy and frustration in the crown of the head or in the forehead, sadness in the throat, fear in the chest, anxiety in the whole musculature and in the racing of our minds and fluttering of our hearts. We can develop the ability to:

- Experience emotions as pure energy; and
- Cultivate, work with and direct that energy.

Being able to notice the physical sensations of emotion in your body begins with lovingly embracing the very sensations you might much rather will away. The first step in this direction is to focus on and deepen the breath. Suppressed, shallow breathing suppresses emotions; deep, conscious breathing lets them flow.

Deepen your breath. Notice where in your body the feelings start to spring up. You can do this exercise even if you don't know how you feel or think you don't have any big emotions right now. Engaging deeply with the gift of your breath will almost always open doors to emotions of which you were previously unaware.

As you breathe into the quality and intensity of any strong emotion, lovingly allow all the accompanying sensations. Gently refuse to attach a label of "good" or "bad" to any of these sensations or the associated emotional states. Remember that every emotion is energy, and that at its core is an expression of greatness. There is no emotion that can't be breathed through you, although some are markedly more challenging to experience than others. (That just means they have greater energy; the energy of a lightning strike, perhaps, compared to the energy of a light bulb.) More energy means more potential as "rocket fuel," as you'll see below.

Choose an especially challenging feeling moment to breathe into whatever you are feeling. Appreciate that you are allowing yourself to feel whatever is there. Acknowledge and experience your frustration, sadness, anger or fear. You are giving yourself the gift of feeling your feelings, including those that are difficult to tolerate. This is a quality of greatness.

Fearlessly as possible, allow yourself to simply feel. Trust that you can handle and circulate strong emotions. Bring your breath right into your heart. Trust that your heart can handle most anything. Acknowledge this quality in yourself as you might acknowledge others when you see even a glimmer of it. Rather than trying to "fix" a feeling in someone else because you judge it to be unpleasant or undesirable, directly appreciate the person for having the courage to really feel:

"I see that a wave of sadness came over you, and that you are giving yourself the gift of feeling it."

"I see your frustration and anger. I am in awe of your wisdom and good judgment. You are handling it without lashing out, even though you might be feeling the impulse. That's great power."

Feel your feelings without getting attached to the story

around them. Your stories matter, but they are in your mind, not your heart or your body, and below the neck is where this energy will circulate. Making a case for feeling angry or sad is a distraction. Surround-sounding feelings with stories from the past and worries about the future can dig you into an energetic hole. Trying to understand or justify and dissect those stories can actually deepen existing grooves of negativity; its usual result is to energize internal negativity.

To make emotions productive, keep the process of feeling and moving that energy simple and sparse: energize your willingness to go into that feeling place fully; allow the feeling itself to be its own pure energy; then, shift that energy to greatness.

Use the energy of your current level of despair and suffering to nourish and propel yourself into greatness. Feel the energy of the feelings come over you like a brief wave, experience them deeply and efficiently, and channel this into ever-growing determination to create the absolute *yes* of greatness.

"I love that I have this feeling and am so alive...I am not taking it out on anyone...and I'm not falling apart." That's huge! Give yourself credit, because you most certainly *could* be falling apart. In recognizing this success, you give yourself the option to compost these very feelings into nutritious thoughts, expressions and actions that can feed your soul and nourish your world.

Later in this book, you will receive more guidance for churning the energy of negativity into compost that will enrich the "soil" that is you. It will come to feel like Miracle-Grow – it will widen your eyes to seeing the greatness that you possess and that has been there all along. You'll even come to see difficult emotions that arise from challenging circumstances – frustration at inequity or injustice, for example – as opportunities to channel energy and to elevate and excite your heart. In such circumstances, you might say to yourself, "I am the greatness of justice and a loving heart." This will inevitably lead to resolutions you would otherwise have never anticipated, and that could not have been possible if you had simply resisted, avoided or squashed down that emotion of frustration.

We are only limited by our imaginations. See how far you can take this. More levels are always available.

# The Bone
## Pile

*Two traveling monks reach a river where they meet a young woman. Wary of the current, she asks if they can carry her across. As their vows forbid them to touch women, one of the monks hesitates; but the other quickly picks her up onto his shoulders, transports her across the water, and puts her down on the other bank. She thanks him and departs.*

*As the monks continue on their way, the one who did not carry the woman is brooding and preoccupied. Unable to hold his silence, he speaks out. "Brother, our spiritual training teaches us to avoid any contact with women, but you picked that one up on your shoulders and carried her!"*

*"Brother," the second monk replies, "I set her down on the other side, while you are still carrying her."*

I found myself in a 'stuck' place with an important person in my life. I desperately wanted to talk it through, reach a place of mutual understanding, and perhaps even get an apology. The other person wanted all of the same things, including an apology from me. The more we talked and delved, the worse the situation became. We had to both see that any amount of talking about the issues was actually putting more gas on what had now grown into a much larger fire. It took tremendous resolve for us to let go of the background noise.

The lesson I learned (yet again, and probably not for the last time) from that experience: You do not have to laboriously deconstruct or reconstruct your life to live in your greatness. You do not have to dissect your past failures and traumas in order to avoid making the same mistakes again.

This assertion runs against much psychological theory and practice, including some of the models in which I was heavily trained as a therapist. It may run counter to fundamental beliefs you hold dear. I'll even assert that going into the bone pile of the past can be the very thing that keeps you on hold with the greatness you are manifesting in this new Now.

Consider the 'Crime Scene Investigation' typically performed in the wake of problems. We often mount a CSI before the dust has even settled following a conflict. This well-intentioned delving is meant to unearth a fix that will heal the damage and prevent a recurrence of the same problem.

Going into CSI mode gives your life energy – your greatest gift – to problems. This very energy contributes to the energetic impression that more connectedness and aliveness arise in times of adversity.

Delving into the past to try to construct the appropriate Now is something like doing manual labor. It arises from a belief that for each error made in the past, you accrue experience and knowledge that you get to apply to your life today. You are locked in at the level compensated per unit of time spent struggling, making mistakes, attempting to figure out how not to make the same mistakes, and suffering.

The greatness practice is more like the entrepreneurial model: income streams with endless possibility for exponential growth. In this model, mistakes are a precious part of the equation that leads to great successes. We wouldn't dream of critiquing a baby's faltering first steps on the way to walking. We don't use those steps as a gauge of that baby's future walking potential! We cheer him on. The same rules apply to energizing each step toward success, including those that feel clumsy or travel in not exactly the direction we will ultimately travel.

We all have the urge to go back and sift through that bone pile – to delve into the archeology of the past to try to understand something that is happening now: a conflict with another person, perhaps, or an internal struggle or unanswered question. But really: what's the expiration date on the past? One minute, one month, one year, a lifetime? Or is it past as soon as it's no longer the present? How long is it okay to hold on to the past? At some point, using any aspect of the past to understand the present just keeps us stuck. This is doubly true when you stay with mistakes, regrets or problems. Putting your energy there removes you from the present moment and all the possibility it holds. Instead, choose to trust that you can use the energy of the emotions that arise around those problems – the fire from the frustration, sadness, or anger – to grow the greatness that is infinitely more likely to get us where we want to go. We can stay inspired to use foresight rather than hanging out in any degree of hindsight.

Ultimately, I have found it harder to let go of the last few seconds than to let go of the stuff from my childhood. But every last ounce of this letting-go of even the last few seconds before this new Now holds a treasure trove of 'fossil fuel' that can power us into the promised land of greatness. This fuel is a match for any other, gallon for gallon – and some of it has *very* high octane.

The present is a natural outgrowth of every moment that has come before. Trying to consciously manipulate the disappeared past and the intangible future will only remove you from the Now, with no guarantee of self-improvement, better relationships or greater happiness.

If you feel the need to process something that has already occurred, hold an intention to reach a solution rather than flailing around in the energized drama of the problem. But keep in mind all you need to resolve your issue is present in this very Now. A massive tree grows to its present state from a tiny seed simply by continually unfolding in the Now. Like that seed, you contain all you need to fulfill your potential and manifest all your greatness in the present.

I maintain that our society has a shared base of WMDs (worries, misery and doubts). All the movies we watch, all the TV and commercials, all the YouTube videos, all the Facebook feeds play along the same themes and dramas. There is no need to discern which fragmented, archetypal, or ancestral WMD should be teased out and tossed in the trash. The content is less important than the context, and the context that matters is the Now.

You don't have to tell your body how to heal a cut. It already has all of the information and intelligence it needs to knit that cut closed as though it never existed. And in the very same way, if you step toward greatness, the greatness within you that has always been in your hardware *(heart-ware)* is activated. Just as that cut knows how to heal, your intelligent soul and spirit know how to access ever-increasing levels of greatness. It's a flow we can enter at any time we choose. We just have to choose it.

If I see a stuck place in my life – within a relationship, for example – I can choose to freak out, lament my situation, get into a CSI, or get overwhelmed with fear and disappear into the cave of WMDs.

I've mostly trained myself to always return to my faith in greatness, which is a native knowing we have, just like the knowing our bodies rely upon to heal cuts. That knowing always brings me back to the present moment. Staying with it and amplifying it is always the first step to real healing.

# House of the
# Rising Sun

I created a greatness meditation in my exploration of releasing the past:

*Imagine greatness to be the ever-expansive ocean of the heart.*

*Imagine the breath as a propeller that stirs this ocean of greatness.*

*Imagine subtle energy coming alive in your heart with each breath.*

*Imagine the rhythm of your heartbeat dancing with each breath, embracing each new moment with love.*

*Then, imagine greatness to be the ultimate 'heart cleanse:'*
*Envision the release of whatever no longer serves you from where it is held in the cells of the heart, body and mind.*
*Allow the pure light of greatness to glow brightly in the ocean of your heart space. Use breath synchronized with heartbeat.\**
*On each in-breath, allow light into the cells of the heart.*
*With each outbreath, allow the exit of all that isn't greatness.*

*Honor the past as fuel for the fire of greatness.*
*Release any worry about discerning and judging what, in your personal or ancestral past, has served or not served.*
*Let it be fuel for the Now. Imagine a big pile of fuel feeding a raging fire that is, in essence, you.*

The day after I first tried this meditation, I woke up feeling so much lighter and softer in my being…and I was thirstier than

---

\* Puran and Susanna Bair's practice of Heart Rhythm Meditation has been a motivating influence in my exploration of synching the breath.

I had ever been. I was thoroughly parched from the inside out. After taking a few big gulps from the faucet, I went out onto the porch adjoining my room to greet the rising sun.

In that moment, I saw that this new version of greatness wasn't so much a raging fire, but the glory of a rising sun: compelling, inspiring, uplifting, and invigorating. It was the kind of light that makes people feel excited about the dawning of a new day.

Later on, I took a yin yoga class that helped me feel more deeply into the heat I experienced in the meditation. In yin yoga, poses are held for a long time – two minutes or more. I felt old, fragmented parts of myself rising to the surface of my consciousness. The experience was something like 'burning off' ancient places and patterns I was holding in my body – patterns I recognized were holding me back. I could feel how the heat generated fuel for the fire of the present moment. At some point, the fire began to feel all-consuming. I touched into what it might feel like to lie in a funeral pyre, but at the same time, I saw that this was the amount of power existing in the light we carry. I felt fearless and beautiful. The feeling went on into the night, and again, I woke from sleep tremendously parched. I couldn't seem to get enough water.

By the next morning, I wondered whether whatever I was doing was more than my body and soul could handle. I went to my balcony to look at the rising sun, and realized that its sweet light was more what I had in mind as a cleansing and releasing fire. The morning sun carries its own moisture with it. It feels so sweet, so life-giving—not all-consuming like the fires I'd experienced in my meditation and yoga practice.

That's when I really understood how this ignition of greatness looks when it catches fire. I internalized the flames of the morning sun and its radiant warmth – the warmth that sustains the whole world without discriminating, reminding us of who we really are. We carry that glimmering sun, always, in our hearts.

# Resetting
# Yourself

*If there is sin against life, it consists... in hoping for another life and in eluding the implacable grandeur of this life.*

— Albert Camus, Nobel laureate novelist and essayist

The word 'sin' comes from a Greek word that means 'missing the mark.' If, for instance, we spend time with or energize negativity, we may be missing the mark in a way that costs us more than meets the eye. We may not be doing outward harm to others, as when we fail to follow the basic tenet of *doing no harm;* but, as Camus so elegantly says, we may be sinning against life. We are finding a space between the ideal and the current reality and moving in there with all of our furniture.

Not only are we 'paying' with our energy for the privilege of the flow of negativity – which, in itself, is wearying and takes its toll – but this same negativity taints our current relationship with self and others. We radiate an upside-down energetic message to the universe: that we like whatever negative thing in which we are choosing to invest our energy. In plowing and fertilizing the field of problems, we reap a harvest. We step into the shared trance where problems bring us the juiciest version of connected relationship. We invest in a space of less-than-great.

The good news is that you can turn this around at any time. You can choose to boldly reframe your life and experiences as expressions of greatness. The first step in this direction is to change the default settings that set you on the unhappy trail into WMDs. This is most easily accomplished through a very simple but life-altering practice called *resetting.* In this practice, you are essentially renewing yourself in light of your greatness: *resetting to who you really are.*

When you catch yourself energizing negativity, take these three steps:

1. **Internally or audibly say "Reset."** In this moment, feel the feelings connected to this issue, problem or negative pull; but choose not to give yourself over to the energy, thoughts, feelings or situation. Efficiently feel and acknowledge what is there, but in that moment of recognition, choose not to give the gift of YOU to the problem or issue.

2. **Pause.** This may require only a few seconds. Take more time if you need it.

3. **Redirect yourself away from negativity and toward some aspect of greatness.** *Use the energy of the negativity* to create a shift into seeing and acknowledging any greatness you can perceive in the moment following the reset. Appreciate the conscious effort you are making and your resourcefulness in having chosen to reset. Appreciate the qualities you possess that have allowed you to resist the pull of negativity. Remember the inspiration of the stories of the Tolltaker, Miracles from Molecules, and Baby Steps.

4. **Repeat as necessary.** Some days, I reset what seems to be a million times. Sometimes, multiple resets are needed around the exact same issue. Each new Now creates space for a new reset about whatever is happening, even if it's the same old issue you have been wallowing in for the last decade! Today, now, you are unplugging yourself from that old issue. You are shifting that pattern in this moment, and that is something to celebrate.

5. **Use the energy of negative emotions as fuel.** Use any shred of emotion that arises from worry, doubt, fear, or other negative feelings as fuel. Lovingly inhabit the feeling. Breathe into it. Know that it is a kind of truth serum that holds vital information. Instead of running from it or trying to get rid of it, allow it to be perfect jet fuel for firing up next levels of greatness.

Every complaint, negative judgment or comment has a positive flip side—a silver lining. Perhaps you are mad at yourself for what feels like a bad decision. What quality of greatness are you feeling that would help your cause? If you are judging yourself as stupid, then underneath that judgment is a belief that you really are intelligent. Energize, though your breath, your greatness of intelligence.

Maybe you feel like complaining about someone else's bad attitude. What ideal are you seeking for your bad-attitude-burdened friend to live up to? Maybe you have a belief that she ought to be more respectful of others. Rather than energizing the lack of that value, find ways in which she is already being respectful. To whatever degree she shows respect, there is that much opportunity to appreciate her respectfulness. *Energize the ideal of what you wanted in the first place.*

The reset is a richly self-nurturing practice. Since a reset is always the only thing between you and your next iteration of greatness, it illuminates each moment as a new opportunity to not just love yourself, but to fall ever more deeply in love with one's self, others, and the world – even if it is just a micro-movement in that direction.

# Skipping the
# Song and Dance

How many times have you gone over and over in your head the reasons why something or someone no longer worked in your life: chips, maybe, or coffee, or not exercising, or a relationship, or a job? How many times did you rehearse the emerging words, then the more perfected words, and then the polished-to-gemlike-sparkle words: a narrative of reasons why you needed to do what you did, in an effort to justify your feelings and actions?

In the process of arriving at those conclusions and refinements, how much energy was poured into those inner conversations? How much of your energy was spent interacting with yourself in this intense and potentially convoluted way? How much of that energy was negative in nature? Did that negativity originate from roots of fear or worry?

You might have been creating a narrative designed to sell your great ideas or qualities. But in that selling, how much of it was the creation of a narrative that emerged though a counterbalance of doubts and anticipated arguments against the proposal, or refutations of what might be others' reasons why your proposal wasn't a good idea? In other words: just how much of what looks like a positive narrative holds seeds of negativity?

This is the human condition. We gravitate toward self-discovery and we try to understand how the world seems to work. We seem to need reasons – reasons that rationalize; reasons that address why; and reasons that move us closer to our dreams. Of course, at times, we have to flesh out our ideas to help others understand what we are communicating, just as I am attempting to do here. It would be ridiculous to go into a meeting at work, put an idea on the table and not be able to explain what it is or why it will be the widget of the future. In the formulation of those very thoughts, it is standard protocol to purposefully include anticipated arguments of those you work with and any thoughts the wider public may bring into the conversation. Of course, we cannot just plop down an idea and say "Because!" and expect anything more than a plop.

But let me also ask you this. When you go for your cup of tea or coffee in the morning, do you make up a narrative about why, or do you just go on a feeling? Many of us might have a narrative running in our heads about why we want a cup of coffee when it's not the best thing for our health, but in situations when you 'know' you want something - when you are simply and purely hungry or tired or needing water or a bathroom break – aren't you clearly overriding the narratives? Don't you simply trust your knowing about the action you are already taking or plan to take?

When we simply 'trust' our 'knowing,' we skip the song and dance. We can, to some extent, reduce or eliminate the pain and agony of potentially draining and enervating inner arguments – the inner conversations that can disrupt our sleep or distract us from the moment with worries, misery and doubts that can clog our systems and interrupt our healthy lives.

Over a period of a few months I had a bird's view of this very issue. I went deep into that place of draining inner conversations over an especially challenging problem in my life. Luckily, I had a process to fall back upon again and again, the process that is the heart of this book; nevertheless, as I look back, I think: *wouldn't it be so lovely someday to so trust myself, to SO love and honor the feelings that inform my mind and heart, to so be keenly aware of the truth serum of my sadness, anger and other emotions, to be so deeply endowed with greatness, that on a personal level of decision-making, I'll be able to skip all the rationalizations and justifications and just know what I need to do, and just trust that it is right, by way of the greatness of my wisdom?*

After all: to a great degree, we all do this already, with issues that don't hold huge importance. We might think that more important issues require more rationalizing and justifying, but ultimately, how helpful is that process in coming to a decision, even about a life or death choice? Having devoted many years now to polishing and honing my growing field of greatness, I find that even issues that once weighed heavily on me are now nearly effortless to navigate, without that song and dance.

I can know what is best for me in the movie that is my life, regardless of whether what I choose is right for anyone else or not. No need for justifications, rationalizations or explanations. End of story. No more need for endless and tiring narratives – especially those that inadvertently perpetuate the very field of negative energy that undermines our health and well-being.

# World-Class
# Complainers

*"Stewardess?"*

*"Yes, sir?"*

*"I want to complain about this airline. Every time I fly, I get the same seat. I can't see the in-flight movie and there are no window blinds, so I can't sleep."*

*"Captain, shut up and land the plane."*

When I was a kid, people would greet one another by saying things like "Well?" or "New?" or "What's up?" ("Well" sounded like "Vell;" "What's up?" sounded like "Vat's up?")

None of these seeming questions were straightforward requests for direct transmission of information. "What's up?" translated energetically to "what's down?" "New?" was actually "What new problems can you share with me today?" As we kids watched adults exchange around this opening, we saw clearly that it really was an invitation to compare miseries: *Who gets more tragedy points today?* "Well" had nothing to do with wellness, either. It referred to the well of problems and despair, which we believed to be the shortest route to potent interpersonal connection.

External relationships based on problems become templates for internal relationship. As these external relationships impact our most present internal dialogue, they give rise to modes such as perseveration, obsessive complaining, bemoaning, worry, doubt and fear. When friends listen to friends who dwell on negativity, it becomes evident on some level that they must love complaints. When we entertain a negative train of thoughts and feelings, then that's the energetic message: that as much as we dread and hate these thoughts, we really love them more than what is right.

Whatever thoughts we think and whatever words we say are the substance of what we inspire to and conspire to. They are a part of what we "feed" our cells, tissues and bodies.

"My colleague at work doesn't turn in his work on time."

"My boss is too bossy."

"My employees are ungrateful."

"After everything I did for my kids, they moved to another town, and they don't come home for holidays."

"I'm fifty and my parents are still trying to run my life."

"That person talks too loud."

"That person doesn't talk loudly enough and I always have to ask her to repeat what she said."

"My everything hurts."

*As bad as world-class complainers are with one another, they are often a hundred times worse with themselves.* You wouldn't say "That person should be fired" more than once or twice in a conversation; but how many of us wouldn't obsessively think the same thought dozens of times – if not hundreds! – over the course of a day when that issue is particularly stuck in our craw?

What friend would put up with worry, fear and doubt bouts half the night, first thing in the morning, even on the toilet and in the shower? That inner voice saying the same darned thing to you, over and over, in so many different ways, provides a glimpse of the quality of friendliness you give to yourself.

Consider this: When's the last time you lost a night's sleep dwelling on what's right, what you are grateful for, or what greatness you find in others? Did your inability to quiet that positive voice in your head keep you awake long into the night?

Giving complaints center-stage airtime in our minds and in the theatre of our souls is like creating a play with the title "I

Love Complaints." The energetic meta-message is that complaints are the best way to have wonderfully alive relationship with self or others, and that's exactly what challenges us in having more fully and wonderfully alive *positive* relationships with ourselves and others. You can't serve two opposing deities without getting caught in the middle.

# Be Here
## KNOWing

R am Dass, the mystic who famously said, "Be here now," speaks of many inspiring experiences of "luminous consciousness" and "polishing the mirror of the heart." Having heard Ram Dass talk on several occasions and deeply respecting several people I know who have been in his life, I feel him as a kindred spirit. Still, although so many hold "be here now" as one of their most sacred insights, it has never quite done it for me.

I feel driven to actualize presence into possibility. I always want to be moving toward and flowing into ever more greatness. Instead of being here *now,* I want to *"be here knowing."* I want to use my intelligence and wisdom to *create* my now instead of being a bystander or a witness.

Someone once called me a practical mystic, because I believe and teach that although there is an absolute beauty to mindfulness and finding the pristine unattached spirit in this moment, within that sacred space is an opportunity to lend greatness to the gift of NOW.

What do I want to *do* with my luminous consciousness? What do you wish to do with yours? Is there a way to steadily and intentionally move in the direction of this consciousness, and to enjoy the glow of each increment of luminosity as we go?

Knowing what I want to do with my Now is my activism. Knowing I want to see and express greatness in each unfolding Now brings its own luminosity of joy. It endlessly inspires next Nows of joyous being.

# Singing
# Your Song

For years now, I've enjoyed opportunities to sing the songs of other people – to introduce them publicly in a way that lights up the runway for others to see them in greatness. Until recently, this was limited to those I viewed in a special light, but I feel I have broken a barrier that has opened me up to singing the song of pretty much anyone and everyone.

One inspired day, I was imagining what it would be like to have all seven billion people currently sharing the earth collectively raise their voices in song. Imagine how great it would be if we all were singing harmonizing songs, or if we were singing the same song. Imagine if it was in celebration of something fantastic, like the beauty of the planet or the magnificence of the universe.

Imagine how great it would be if all of these seven billion people not only were singing, but were singing with heart. Think of all the glorious souls bursting out in song in glorious unison.

Now, a little science: Most scientists say our bodies are comprised of somewhere between 10 and 75 trillion cells; the last estimate I spotted was 35 trillion. Imagine, now, transposing this same image of heartfelt, soul-shining song to the universe that is within each of us. Imagine that seven billion of the cells in your body had the shining faces and souls of those currently living on the planet – maybe those particular seven billion cells that comprise your heart. Maybe the other cells could represent the many other living beings of the plant and animal kingdom, large and small: no-legged, two-legged and more-legged, flying, swaying, swimming; and these great and varied beings were represented by the other amazing tissues, muscles, and organs of our bodies. Imagine then all these great beings singing YOUR song, in praise of the universe that is YOU. Imagine these cells singing in unison and singing their hearts out, singing your name.

Our bodies require magnificent diversity of form and function to be at peak health and performance. Imagine how this recognition and this meditation on this universe within you, a universe as marvelous and complex as the entire universe in which we live, might impact the way you see everyone from here on out.

Imagine that every being is already singing songs of celebration, whether to their daily tasks, their faith, their beliefs, their sports heroes, their possessions, what they cherish, or what they choose to bless with their own unique energies. Even though many such endeavors might contrast or even clash with yours, imagining that all beings are also cells within one's own universe helps us to cherish whatever song is being sung by anyone.

Even if other singing beings look rough around the edges, they are singing, just like you. Make room for them in your ensemble. As an orchestra leader, how would you lead them to play harmoniously? Maybe it's as easy as imagining them singing your song.

When I choose to hold this point of view, I don't want to write off, dismiss, or discriminate against different parts of my body – my universe. I want all parts singing. In this context, having an issue with even one 'kind of being,' for whatever reason, is commensurate with writing off differing kinds of tissues, cells or organs or functions within me. War without is war within.

I don't want to engender any such kind of loss of form or function within myself or in the world I live in. I want all aspects of form and function to work collaboratively and harmoniously together.

This entire great creation that is our universe must have sprung forth from some kind of imagination. We have been given the greatness of imagination—one of the gifts of all gifts. Maybe all great things begin in our imaginations. Why not imagine this inspiring chorus of multitudes of voices rising together? I can't see a single reason why I should stop imagining having my song sung, or why I should stop singing yours.

# The First
# Community

Take three breaths.

Now, consider: how *not* great would it be if you weren't breathing, or if your breathing were hampered? Ever seen someone who doesn't breathe well? *Not* fun. If that's not you, today – what a miracle that you're breathing normally!

The breath is the only body function that is both autonomic (happens whether we consciously do it or not) and controllable (we can manipulate the breath, making it longer, shorter, faster, slower, deeper, shallower, or hold it for a period of time). We can also use the breath as a vehicle of conveyance—a way to move energy around in the body in concert with specific thoughts and words. You can do the greatness practice with just your mind, but when you use the breath to deepen it into the rest of your body, it has much greater power. Defaults shift more quickly and more readily stick in their new settings when body and mind are drawn together with words and breath.

The body is the first community. Its trillions of cells are the citizens of this community. The movement of inspired spirit in the form of breath passes first to the cells; only then can this spirit move beyond the cells to the community at large. Breathing consciously into greatness and circulating this energy throughout the body prepares us to manifest the fullness of who we are into the larger community.

For me, yoga is simply a way of actively moving the greatness of breath through the body. Yoga and breath work help move "issues in the tissues" into opportunities. The energy stored as these issues can be 'wells' (like oil wells) where we can figuratively drill down to recover/recycle stored emotions to use as jet fuel for greatness. The very issues that fossilize in bones, muscles and tissues as fat, sclerosis, arthritis and such can become fossil fuel that propels our greatness to fruition and purpose. Yoga and breath potentialize this movement, giving us the ability to capture this vast energy and make it useful rather than detrimental.

Go ahead and love your body because it works: because it walks, breathes, digests, eliminates, and has a working immune system. Imagine if any of these physiologic functions went on even partial hiatus. What if your eliminative systems decided only to work while you were sleeping? So, so very *not* great.

Make a new habit of experiencing and appreciating your body. Start by taking at least one slow, conscious breath. Feel how this feels in your pelvic floor, your low belly, your mid-belly, your chest, your neck, your face, the top of your head. Scan around. What are your toes up to right now? Do they like the shoes you're wearing, or do they want to be set free to burrow into the rug? How about the palms of your hands? Your thighs? Your liver? Your kidneys?

Your body loves to have the light of your awareness and gratitude shone upon its many parts. Visit with it as you would visit with a cherished friend. Check up on it and express your gratitude and love for it. Move loving breath through it; send the energy of greatness on your breath anywhere in your own body that is calling out for extra honoring and love.

If we want to influence the communities we live in or have those communities be more at peace and more harmonious and collaborative, how can we inspire our first community to do the same? Do we suppress our bodies' indications that we need greater love and collaboration, or do we find a way to give our communities of cells and systems what they need?

We can provide vast love and honoring through positive thoughts, sent out through the great vehicles of breath and movement. This can be achieved through a yoga practice, or through other practices that unite body and intention. Any such practice holds the potential to move through level after level of greatness.

This has been my sincere quest for several years now. The more I seem to inspire my body through positive messages, the further I want to take the exploration and the better I get at feeling the impact of strong and subtle emotions and negativity. Through each next unfolding, I become more energized and challenged in refining messages of greatness.

# Greatness Breathing:
# An Introduction

The Nurtured Heart Approach is immersed in life, not separate from it. It is embedded in relationship; it is not simply a vision or theory or philosophy of how things should be, but rather a way of being. And Greatness Breathing is, by its nature, a full immersion as well. As long as we are alive, we are never not breathing. Breathing is already a context for everything and anything we do and all we are. It is a perfect conveyance of life force. On its airwaves can ride a transmission of whatever thoughts we choose as nourishment.

This is not a practice for which we need to carve out 10 or 20 minutes a day. Having the time to practice Greatness Breathing is a given, because we are already always breathing, just as we are already always great. We are in the process of remembering and awakening what is already there, inspiring and igniting it. In doing so, we are already doing Greatness Breathing and the greatness practice.

The mere act of breathing, whether shallow or deep, is one of creating life, giving back to the universe (plants use the carbon dioxide we generate for sustenance), and converting the energy we generate to the fire of life: activities of the day and efforts to support our intentions and purpose. So we are already the greatness of transforming energy, giving and creating – it is inherent even in our breathing.

We allow ourselves, moment to moment, to receive the gift of breath: this oxygen, air, *prana,* energy that the in-breath conveys. This in-breath sustains us, but in any next moment, it could shift into the lack of this life-giving energy. Obviously, life ends at that point. No guarantee exists that any next breath will come.

Moving through life with that recognition also requires the greatness of trust: trusting that this most tenuous life-and-death, omnipresent process is worth it all. In this trust, we risk sleeping, exercising, and other activities that could jeopardize that fragile life – things we wouldn't do if we didn't trust our next breath would indeed be there. And so we have the greatness of courage: because if we didn't, we wouldn't risk even getting out of bed in the face of such uncertainty.

To begin your Greatness Breathing practice, notice that you are already breathing, and see each breath for what it truly is: a miracle. And then, recognize that breathing alone demonstrates that we have qualities of courage, trust, and being receptive. All of these qualities require love and compassion – more greatness. So the greatness of being is a given, and the greatness of breath is a given.

# Breathing
# the Reset

We are going to get to our greatness inevitably, anyway, at some point – in one minute, one hour, one day, one month, one year, one lifetime, or one hundred lifetimes. If we are going to get that great state of being *no matter* what, then why not give it our all, right now? Why not rise to that occasion in this very moment?

Even better: if I notice that I'm not quite doing that, I can use the frustration of "not-quite-being-there-now" as jet fuel for next levels of greatness. If I am destined to work out an issue, I'll keep magnetizing experiences towards me that will help me do that. That's how the universe works. So I may as well see each hurdle, each issue, as holding that kind of fuel, and keep converting and alchemizing it in service to greatness.

Even the most efficient conversion of the jet fuel of WMDs leaves a residue of negativity – traces of that energy lingering in the body, heart and mind. Recognizing this and respecting it leads us to strike a loving balance of continually releasing negative energy from every cell of our being so that energy does not then get stuck and interfere with our ability to be present.

Here's a process to help you continually move this energy of negativity:

1. Feel the feeling. Refuse to get pulled in, but also refuse to freak out and push the feeling down. When you feel negativity float in, give yourself the gift of lovingly feeling it. If you feel a strong charge in the feeling, use the energy as jet fuel to propel any related next levels of greatness that will help bring you to what your being is calling into form. Call up qualities of greatness that will help you be fully ready for situations like this next time around the block.

2. Once you breathe these next levels of greatness into your cells – into the community of you – take time to acknowledge any leftover traces of energy related to the negativity that stimulated this round of growth. Be willing to gently, lovingly breathe these through and out. Use your breath to release any negativity and traces of negative energies and memories, fully cleansing your cells and spirit.

This loving process will help you continually awaken to your true being. It will help you to remember and engage your growing greatness, which is just waiting to be remembered so that it can call you into action.

# Primal
# Nutrition

As I intentionally build my own greatness, I find new love and reverence for my own body. I want to get rest and I want to play. I accept my body exactly as it is, at every age and stage; and I recognize that wishing for some part of my younger self means I am living in the past – cause for a reset and return to greatness. I want to do yoga most every day and to nourish my body with healthy food. I love how my body supports my quests and responds when I treat it well. I love how it reminds me of what is damaging to it by challenging me when I consume too much of anything that it braces against or that challenges its well-being.

Many of the foods now considered "addictive" have the effect of whetting our appetites without offering any real nutrition. Some regard this as a kind of evil being inflicted upon us by greedy food conglomerates. I prefer to see it as yet another way the generous universe offers guidance. Empty, over-flavored, over-sugared, over-salted food can bring us back to remembering our longing for the primal nutrition of food grown in nutrient-rich soils and prepared with intention and love. Food devoid of nutrition creates an addictive pattern until we awaken to the path back to what truly nourishes us.

When I open a bag of chips and start compulsively eating them, my body, in its infinite wisdom, is in effect scanning, scanning, scanning each chip and reporting back to my brain: "No nutrition." On I go, downing chip after chip, and I can go on like that for a long time.

If I stop, reset, and proceed to mindfully consider thoughts pertaining to greatness, putting the chips away is suddenly the only logical thing to do. Giving myself real soul-level nutrition as a substitute for empty nutrition removes the vacuous allure of the salty snack.

When I first recognized this dynamic in myself, I became inspired to try eating foods with real nutrition. I was led to a person who had great knowledge about food healing, and because of the greatness work I have done over the years, I was ready to take in her profound wisdom when I encountered her. I asked her to teach me more about what she knew and offered to have a class at my home. She said she could do a class for no fewer than five people, including me. Within minutes of my putting the word out, four great friends signed up.

When we gathered, she explained how plant foods are loaded with complex chemicals – phytochemicals – that are nourishing to our bodies in multiple ways. Then, she taught us about micronizing whole plant foods in a high-powered blender. Doing so, she said, would release the 'light energy' and phytochemicals within the food's cells. Including seeds in the mix was important too, because seeds hold great wisdom and intelligence that are released during high-speed blending of whole foods. She told us that as we finally give the body this pure level of nutrition, it will respond with its own wisdom, letting us know what it needs with progressive clarity.

Like the cut that heals itself, the body in relation to progressively better attunement to greatness will tell you more and more what it really needs to manifest even more greatness. I delighted in finding that even a small amount of powerfully nutrient-dense food catapulted me to a new realm of not needing or wanting foods with lesser nutrition. I still eat chips now and then, but I do so strictly for enjoyment. It's no longer compulsive, and it is no longer a substitute for the power of real foods. Since shifting to this micronized whole foods approach, I find it easy and natural to consume mostly pure food. I eat a fraction of what I used to, because my body instantly recognizes that it is getting what it needs. I don't have to try to not to want the foods that don't support me in a core way. That wisdom is simply there.

# Greatness Blessing for
## a Healthful Meal

*Thank you for the love and light pouring through the elements of the wind, air, and earth.*

*Thank you for the warmth of the sacred fire of the sun, pouring into the beings of the soil, the vines, and the branches, into these brimming conveyances of spirit that nourish us.*

*Thank you for the way this pure light energy amplifies itself as it moves through us, reminding us daily of who we really are.*

*Thank you for making us hunger in an ongoing way for these conveyances of spirit, and for our ongoing hunger to be the embodiment of that spirit.*

*Thank you for the primal nutrition of greatness that deeply nourishes us.*

*Amen.*

# The Dance of the
# "Many Mes"

Most people define themselves in terms of their roles in life: parent, spouse, employee, student, employer, entrepreneur, athlete, lover, teacher…and the list takes off from there.

Your roles reflect what is important to you. They can reflect what you love and where you wish to put your energy. Some roles seem to choose us; ideally, we choose the majority. Some roles carry more importance or feel more like who we think we really are, but hopefully, they all reflect our core values and beliefs.

If we go deeper, we can recognize other "roles" we play, which we could also call "personas." I, for example, have an inner guru who loves to wax poetic about greatness work and its spiritual implications. When I sit down to write, he takes the fore and lives large. I also have an inner *kvetch,* who can get cranky if he feels crossed. Then there's the inner romantic, who daydreams about true love; and my inner lone wolf, who enjoys solitude and the freedom to make all my own choices without having to check in with anyone else about anything. Within us there are many of these personas, and they occasionally can be at odds with each other. But what I've found is that they can all coexist in the field of greatness.

I'm new every day. I choose only one definition, one limitation: a life of seeing and creating greatness. Everything else is fluid. Any one of my "many mes" can come out to dance and play in greatness at any time.

There is no safer place to surrender limitations than at the doorstep to greatness. With that surrender comes surprise and delight at all the roles I can play. I don't lose myself as I spread myself wider, because the foundation of greatness underlies it all.

My roles evolve and change as I keep returning to gratitude and greatness. In the rare instances where I am disappointed with an interaction or situation, I use that feeling as fuel – an impetus for stepping into an ever-greater next Now.

Who are you today? Who were you five minutes ago? Who do you want to be in this next Now? *The only "given" about who you are is greatness.* All other aspects of who you are can shift and change – sometimes, dramatically. As you let greatness guide you, see how it feels to let go of your attachment to limiting beliefs about what is possible for you. Let that greatness be your anchor; allow your "many mes" to playfully and earnestly engage with your world.

# "It's Not a Question of Whether You Can or You Can't.
## You Are."

In the film *The Horse Whisperer,* Grace, a girl of about 13, suffers a terrible accident while horseback riding with her best friend. The friend and the friend's horse are killed, and one of Grace's legs has to be amputated. In an effort to bring the girl out of a deep depression, her mother brings Grace and her traumatized horse to Tom, a 'horse whisperer' who she hopes will help both her daughter and her horse recover.

One day, Tom calls Grace out of the stable and offers to teach her how to drive his pickup truck. She protests that she's too young, she can't because of her leg, and so on. But Tom calmly eggs her on until she's in the driver's seat of the truck with the motor running.

"Go ahead and give it some gas," he tells her. She does, and the truck lurches forward. "Now you know you can," he tells her. "Now you just gotta figure out how much." She tries again. Soon the truck is chugging along. "Now just keep driving until you run out of road," Tom tells her, adding, "I think I'll just close my eyes for a little while." He pushes the brim of his Stetson down over his eyes, folds his arms across his belly, and pretends to settle in for a nap.

"But...I don't think I can," Grace feebly protests.

"It's not a question of whether you can or you can't. You are," Tom replies.

In moments where you are at an edge, wishing you could do better or express some quality you think you don't already express, remember this story. Horse Whisperer moments convert "I wish" or "I want" into "I am" or "you are." This alchemic conversion awakens the greatness of the truth of the moment. Like Grace, you might think you *aren't* or you *can't;* but if you develop the

X-ray vision Tom employs, you learn to see – in any moment – how, in some way, you already *are*. Helping ourselves claim that truth propels us into a dimension of claiming the greatness in anything.

I may think I struggle to be respectful; but the truth is, I already am respectful at times. I need to step up and breathe in the truth that I already have that greatness in my being. In owning it, I then can breathe it further into the inner realms of my mind, heart and spirit. It becomes that much more sacred. The trajectory instantly changes. If, in contrast, I choose to remain in the negative perception and perseveration that "I am not respectful enough," I continue to perpetuate energy and relationship around disrespect. Disrespect continues to be a way I connect with self and others.

Apply your great creativity to seeing how, in this very moment, you *are* embodying and living out whatever quality, skill or achievement you yearn for. If you weren't, you wouldn't be at the level of awareness required to want it in the first place. From this same vantage point, you couldn't admire a quality in anyone – someone you know personally or someone you've read or heard about – unless you had enough of that very quality to understand and perceive it. So you already *are* that quality, and it will grow as you consciously and purposefully breathe into and energize it. To the degree that you are already "being" those qualities, *I applaud you! It's not a question of whether you can or you can't. You are.*

# Choose
# Greatness

Over seven billion of us live on this earth. We are well on our way to eight billion. How can we see greatness in one another while experiencing it in ourselves – whether it is hidden, emerging or fully blossomed – and how can we help it emerge further in one another? How can we nurture it along? Begin with yourself. Be the best emerging greatness/godness you can at any moment, and keep listening ever more minutely. Keep choosing to love yourself and keep aligned to your guidance – no one else's – and keep asking for more.

You are always choosing. You are never *not* making a choice, one way or another. Either you are choosing to listen and follow "directions" or "your guidance," or you are choosing to not listen, to not follow. Observe ever more closely and own it all, everything you do or don't do, as a choice. Take ownership of who you are choosing to be in every moment. The more you choose consciously, the more you can be *who you really are.*

Do you want to avoid the magnitude of your greatness and all the guidance leading to that greatness? It's easy enough to put blinders on, to dance and backpedal away from greatness, to refuse to give it your level gaze and pretend it's not for you. You can look away from the sheer scope and level of who you *really* are, or you can begin, to one degree or another, to own it, to breathe it; and then, to engage in an ongoing practice of *living* it. It's understandable that you might be a bit shaken by the illumination you carry: your light takes some degree of getting used to. Gradually, your capacity to look straight at that light will expand, and from there, you can amp up the lumens.

Our culture likes it when we deny our greatness, our majesty, our *God-ness.* When we consider ourselves to be "less-than," we stay in a mode of competition with one another. We can sometimes feel shamed in our culture for loving ourselves. Believing that we are already not only "enough," but that we *have greatness,* and saying so to the world, tends to elicit feedback that we are wrong, misguided, heretic, blasphemous, grandiose, pathological, big-headed or historically worthy of being beheaded. Buying into any level of what can be surround-sound messages of "never enough" and "you can always do/look/be better" makes it easy to pull the plug on any moves forward in greatness. Even if the world doesn't challenge us when we stand in our greatness, many of us are quite gifted at taking the lead in that quest. Do you habitually take yourself down a few notches so no one else has to? If so, you're certainly not alone.

Being in love with yourself means treating all circumstances that come your way with a loving heart. So many circumstances flow in and out of each person's life and consciousness; can we feel and experience it all without abandoning ourselves? And can we achieve this while breathing it all in, in love? Can we *refuse* to exit the stage of appreciation and gratitude for each and every feeling and experience (even those that are most challenging)? This is what it is to be truly *in love* with one's self. That state of love is what enables us to extract the gold/greatness/God-ness from it all. That's the alchemy. That's the magic.

In actuality, stepping truly into our greatness – *who we really are* – and owning it more and more fully makes us more and more human, more full, more soft and available to life, yet more empowered. We become increasingly more aligned to the ever-greater truth of what works and what doesn't, and we can then live in ever-greater clarity. We become more empowered to live life without fear; to be more fully open and to listen more minutely. We become increasingly supportive of humanity rather than taking the fearful stance of detachment and self-absorption.

Imagine that this story is the truest story: that it is our privilege to be within the context of our very own bodies, our very own appearances, our very own thoughts, purpose and mission...our very own moment-to-moment impetus and inspiration. Giving this away – dimming its light, shutting it down – is the only bad choice we can possibly make. And if we recognize ourselves doing this at any point, all we need to do is reset to greatness.

# Dive
# Deep

Being in your greatness does not mean happy-go-lucky all the time. It means being authentically and exactingly true to wherever you are. I am not suggesting that anyone should ignore suffering – our own or others'. The reset is not meant as a bypass around difficult emotions. It is not the magical key to being happy all the time.

Case in point: I am writing this following an evening that might best be described as despairing. I absolutely had thoughts like, "Is this all worth it?"

The universe will magnify what we don't acknowledge. The key is to dive deep, then release. No matter what arises, we will have to face what is and release it. Feelings will come and go; that's okay – they're just feelings. Let them come, be with them, breathe with them, feel them deeply with a loving heart, and see what greatness is called up in response. Know that you will rise to the occasion of whatever it is. Dive deep, then release, and in that moment following – like the moment after a wave has crashed, or a bolt of lightning has struck – see what greatness is called up in response.

If you are feeling despair, can you let yourself really feel it? Can you love yourself in the midst of it? Can you honor your own internal guidance about how to be in those moments without going off the rails? And if you do fall off those rails, can you get back to who you really are - maybe even an ever more determined version?

I am not suggesting that you ruminate or persevate on an issue or the despair you might feel in response to that issue. I am suggesting that you adopt a willingness to experience the fullest truth you can tolerate, so that you can then extract the 'truth serum' from within that deep experience.

Difficult moments are opportunities to nurture your heart to an ever-greater version of who you really are. They carry potent primal nutrition: the kind of compost that can only come from exactly the experiences you have been given. The energy of despair and the energy of ecstasy, and the energy of everything in between, will feed the seeds of greatness and make them grow.

At a lunch meeting with a new consultant, he mentioned that he had just returned from a yoga retreat in Costa Rica. One unexpected bonus of that trip, for him, was that he felt nourished by the food at a level way beyond anything he had ever felt before. This made sense to me: that food was a product of soil deeply enriched by eons of pure, organic compost – soil that was many times richer in nutrition than washed-out, nutrient-depleted American soil. To me, this was a perfect metaphor for the 'inner composting' of all our experiences into a similarly nutrient-rich primal soil that feeds our souls with the rich vitality of greatness: *primal nutrition.*

# Splendor
# Into Form

Although we have not been at a loss for words to express our disdain, disappointment, criticism, revulsion, resignation, and other in-depth arenas and views of negativity, we've culturally been at a loss for words for positive expressions of our loving hearts. The moment has come to transform that.

So many people's primary frustration in life is that they have at least a trace sense of the greatness of their being and the greatness of the love in their hearts. So many of us default to variations on the theme of not being able to even come close to expressing what is there. I have found that giving people an awakening sense and feeling of that greatness and an expanded way of seeing it changes everything.

Lighting up the runway with ways of expressing what they see and feel in words that seem right and doable is an important aspect of this, and those specifics are laid out in the next section of this book. With this first section, I hope to have supported you in a new view of *splendor,* of the greatness that is accessible to you in this very moment. Section Two will continue to move that splendor into form, giving shape and structure to this new trajectory by offering specific techniques and practices. This is my life work: bringing splendor into form.

In the trainings I give, I have seen time and again that when people learn to use the language that accesses that realm, there is no restraining them in expanding it to suit their own trajectories to greatness. It feels right as rain. The dry spell ends. As that rain hits the ground running, blossoms of next iterations of exploration begin to emerge.

Part Two
# Practice

*Is the life I'm living the life that wants to live in me?*

- Parker Palmer

# What's
# Up?

Notice, again, the more or less constant running conversation you conduct with yourself. What is that conversation like? Our next task together is to dig into intentionally transforming that running commentary—to shift from either negativity or traditional positivity to radical positivity.

First, let's define "traditional positivity," because it's all over the worlds of psychology and pop culture, and it differs from our aims here. When we tell ourselves "good job" or we thank ourselves for some deed well done, we are being positive, yes; but we are missing out on an enormous swath of what is possible. An infinite storehouse of radically appreciative potential exists all around us at any given moment, and our task in this section of the book is to equip you to see, acknowledge, and expand upon traditional ideas of positivity.

It will be something like putting on a pair of glasses that transforms and enhances everything you see. Those glasses also magically enhance all your other senses, too—how you hear, how you sense through touch—and the relationships you can build with other people. Forget Google Glass; these greatness lenses are only limited by the power of your imagination and the depth of your heart and spirit. And you don't need a wi-fi connection or a charger to keep them going.

Most people move through the world with little awareness of their self-talk and its gravitational pull to all that is negative. We can easily think that the narrative we're weaving is objective reality rather than subjective storytelling. Noticing that we create it is the first step to transforming it.

One of the biggest challenges adults face in applying the techniques of the Nurtured Heart Approach to children in their lives is their own conditioning. Most adults were raised with traditional disciplinary approaches. These conventional vantage points deeply condition us to put far more energy toward what's going wrong than what's going right. Most parenting theories, practices and philosophies still come down to this upside-down energy. And when push comes to shove – when we get challenged – most adults place more energy and emphasis into criticism and judgment over what's frustrating and worrisome than into seeing how they and others are remarkable and successful.

If we respond to successes armed only with meager and vague responses like "good job" and "thank you," and then we unleash a truckload of emotional and cognitive processing for the issues and challenges we face, energetically, we are still swimming in negativity. If we don't quite see and reach for greatness but get drawn into problem after problem that needs fixing, the gravity of negativity still has a hold on us until we consciously choose otherwise.

If you consider yourself to be a relatively positive person, consider right now the "charge" or level of energy you give to worries, miseries and doubts. Is it qualitatively stronger than the energy you give to your own successes? Are you qualitatively more available and vivid, more emotionally demonstrative, when something's wrong than when things are going along smoothly? How different are you when things aren't going wrong? When you are "catching up" with friends, what parts of the conversation get the most excited levels of exchange? When you are alone with yourself, which aspects of your life get more charged inner dialogue and more playtime?

Most of us are more present and 'alive' when we are faced with problematic thoughts or events than when we are pleased with something positive. In response to the good stuff, we are relatively low-key. We delve into problems with gleeful abandon while often barely acknowledging successes or expressing gratitude.

It can be hard for us to even see successes. We evolved to hone in on problems. Whether we believe in evolution or not, we have to admit that once upon a time, many generations ago, our ancestors had to avoid predators in order to survive. This was a matter of species preservation, and we wouldn't be here now if this did not exist in our ancestors. It wasn't prudent for them to wait until a predator was upon them to make the urgently important decision to flee or to fight; they needed to sense out any tiny increments of danger – any small hint that something was possibly headed their way.

Fast-forward a few hundred thousand years. We're still great at seeing tiny increments of what's wrong, and in our drama-saturated, media-saturated universe, our shared DNA coding for hyper-alertness to what's wrong with the picture has led to new fascinations with/manifestations of gravity pulling toward negativity. These fascinations and manifestations are sometimes subtle and sometimes obvious, and overall, they demonstrate how wired we still are to see, microscopically, what's wrong with the picture. Look up from this page right now. How many things can you find wrong or less than right with your surroundings? Things that could be improved or upgraded? With people nearby? With the setting? With yourself?

We still have remnants of that fear-based brain that gets called into action at the drop of a hat. And when it engages, we are so talented at waxing poetic over what we perceive as wrong. We can go on and on almost effortlessly, the momentum building, fortifying the arguments we make in favor of how the situation needs to be fixed.

In comparison: how well do we launch the argument for what is already going right? How vivid, brilliant and emotionally charged are our positive comments? What recognitions do we make for what is done right?

Do you think that acknowledging your own successes somehow makes you egotistical or arrogant? Do you silently wait and hope for others to acknowledge your successes and feel bereft when they don't? Would you like to know how to acknowledge them and yourself in a way that would propel all into a greatness frame of mind?

I have developed some simple techniques that can help you talk to yourself in a way that makes you your own greatest fan – and, at the same time, the greatest fan of others. (There's no shortage of greatness to go around; ultimately, your greatness enhances rather than diminishes mine, so no need for competition.) Instead of being sidetracked, thrown, upset, confused, blaming or depressed when things go wrong, you can go to greatness and give yourself or others a new chance at success in any next moment.

Beneath the words, beneath the stories we tell ourselves, flows an underground river of energy. Dialing into that energy will lead you to feel into its truth. Begin to notice both the words and the energy flowing beneath your narratives, and those of others. The greatness practice is not about shifting the words or the energy that lies beneath them. It shifts both.

# The Three
# Stands

The Three Stands provide a fallback set of 'guidelines' that move the intentions of the first section of this book into action. As you explore the following three Stands, your default settings will begin to shift.

Stands give power to our clarity in life through two vantage points. A stand is both (1) a refusal – a gift growing clarity regarding what we will no longer permit; and (2) a gift of commitment to growing clarity about what we now want to propel and will now choose to grow.

Here are the three stands of the Nurtured Heart Approach:

### Stand One: Absolutely NO!
*I will not energize negativity.*

Observe your world from the point of view of energy. Watch how you respond. Notice that when you give your energy to an obstacle, you energize it. Refuse to go there. Choose progressive clarity around a refusal to give the gift of yourself to problems, issues or anything negative. Reset yourself whenever negativity arises.

Imagine a toaster. Not just any toaster: this is the most incredible toaster ever made. It not only toasts to perfection, it butters your bread and it even grinds your coffee beans and makes your morning coffee just how you like it. Whatever features you'd most want in a toaster, this one has them. It's the best toaster ever.

See that toaster in your mind's eye. Then, imagine what happens when you unplug it. It doesn't do a thing. Even though it still is the best toaster ever, with all these amazing features, when unplugged it becomes uninteresting and useless. It won't respond to any of your inputs or demands.

This is exactly what happens when you reset yourself. None of your bells and whistles work. None of your features activate, no matter how hard you try. You don't go into action mode until you're "plugged back in" at the completion of the reset.

When negativity arises, consciously choose to take the stand of unplugging. Stay unplugged until you feel reset; then, choose to plug back in by consciously choosing thoughts of greatness.

Greatness plugs that miracle toaster back into its power source. Unplug as many times as necessary. Once you feel reset, plug back in by way of the second stand:

### Stand Two: Absolutely YES!
*I will relentlessly energize and nurture greatness in myself and in others.*

Invoke a fierce commitment to fostering, deepening and propelling greatness wherever possible. Proactively do so by seeing and reflecting greatness all around you, within yourself and as expressed by others. Also do so in the wake of every reset away from negativity. Taking this stand is tantamount to a refusal to forget who you really are as a person of greatness.

Fill the space once occupied by negativity with deeply appreciative, nourishing, energizing true statements reflecting the greatness you now claim. The space created by Stand One is crucial to building the foundation of Stand Two. Ground those statements in your own actions and interactions, thoughts and feelings, and remember: miracles from molecules!

Finding even a tiny glimmer of greatness in yourself or your actions is the prerequisite for growing that greatness.

Don't be intimidated. You will learn all you need to know in order to become an endless source of such statements in coming chapters.

For now, even if specific words of greatness fail to come, set your intention on greatness. Keep returning there until it becomes your default, whether you need to reset back to that space once, twice, or a million times.

**Stand Three: ABSOLUTELY CLEAR!**
*I refuse to let it slide when I cross the line into negativity.*
*I will actively remember to reset, and to use the energy of*
*negativity as an impetus to go further into greatness.*

Reset *every time* you slip into negativity. Hold this mindset: that you will reset eventually, anyway, so the sooner, the better; and the clearer your intention, the better.

This practice does not demand perfection. Negativity will surface. That is a given. Each time it does, see it as an opportunity to choose to efficiently feel the connected emotions and to efficiently receive the truth inherent in your concerns. (Your instinctual knowing comes most easily through the 'truth serum' of your feelings.) Then, choose to efficiently roil and work that negativity to create rich compost for greatness. As you learn to move that energy, you become more fluid with that movement. Embrace resets. Welcome them. Every reset is a gateway to more greatness.

# Active
# Recognition

Not sure where to begin in upholding these stands—in particular, not sure how to find and energize greatness instead of negativity (Stand Two)? The next several chapters will introduce you to four techniques geared to vastly expand your ability to uphold the Second Stand.

The first section of this book was more about the "why"; this section is about the "how." It will help you begin to see the power words hold for shaping the way you perceive yourself and the way you relate to others. You will learn to go from simple, vague, limited language of praise to detailed, specific language of appreciation.

Words are transmissions of energy. Whether you think them inwardly or say them outwardly, they are important conveyors of relationship and of what you energize as meaningful and valued. They can be superficial or they can weigh in deeply, at the soul level. If you let them carry that weight, they can be sacred and magical.

These are "voice-over" techniques that enable you to *catch yourself in successes* and (more importantly) *create successes* at any moment. They are tools for channeling your self-talk toward building inner wealth; they help you effectively and honestly appreciate yourself at an extraordinary level – to give yourself positive, evidence-based reflections deriving from and arriving within your heart and your ever-deepening character. You learn to notice and nurture yourself not only for what you accomplish, *but for who you are.*

There will be people and circumstances that will threaten to abrade your courage and your will, dim your light and dampen your power. I used to fear this until I realized that *no one but me is in charge of my spirit and greatness.* Even in the presence of negativity, I can say to myself, "I'm going to take this negative energy and use it as jet propulsion back into further positivity." Instead of getting into a mindset of trying to figure out what I am doing wrong, how I've done it better in the past, or how I can emulate past successes by walking in those same footsteps, I choose to trust in the moment and expect to inhabit greatness there.

You can create successes with a simple shift in perspective – by seeing that *you are already successful* in so many ways. Stretch your imagination wide to create an exciting vision of the Now, which then sets your expectations for the next Now. Explore the power of your imagination to find ever more detailed, fascinating and subtle permutations of greatness in yourself and others, progressively opening the door to more of the same.

Self-talk happens. It happens more or less constantly. You can see this as a burden, a source of negativity and inner criticism; or you can proactively use it as a tool for shining light on as many successes as you can see, be they miniscule, moderate or immense. You can direct that self-talk toward building inner wealth. Active Recognitions are the simplest and perhaps the most powerful of all these self-recognition, self-acknowledgment techniques.

To give yourself an Active Recognition, give yourself a verbal "snapshot" of what you observe yourself doing. Only observe; do not judge or evaluate.

Reflect your own actions back to yourself as though you were describing them in a voice-over or to a blind person. The most basic aspect of a this type of recognition is pure narration of what 'is.'

"I'm washing the dishes carefully to make sure these delicate pieces are not broken."

"I'm sitting in traffic and feeling mostly calm."

"There's a lot of distracting noise around me right now and I'm staying pretty focused most of the time."

"I am trying to assemble this toy for my son. Not as simple as I thought, but it's fun to see his anticipation."

Active Recognitions draw you into the present moment by grounding you in whatever is *actually happening,* here and now. Simple acknowledgements like these help you begin to recognize and intentionally direct your inner voice—the self-talk that goes on pretty much all the time, whether you pay attention to it or not. You begin to practice shaping inner conversations in ways that shift you to a more positive way of being.

Play with this for a while, until Active Recognitions become a habit. Then, play with more complex versions, boosting positive self-recognitions by acknowledging relevant details.

"I'm washing the dishes right now, even though I don't want to and was nervous about how delicate they are. I'm even sort of getting into it."

"I feel annoyed about having to sit in this traffic jam but I am staying surprisingly calm. It's actually kind of fun entertaining myself by watching the other drivers."

"My mood and focus seem pretty good right now despite a lot of distracting noise. I seem to be able to heighten my concentration on demand, which is pretty fascinating."

"I am trying to assemble this toy for my son, and so far I am staying patient and carefully following directions. It really is amazing and enjoyable to stay present with this and with him while this is getting done."

Some might say that this kind of positivity feels false or contrived. But all you're doing is noticing the truth of your actions, emotions or moods without fixing or altering them. You are choosing to notice what is good; what is going well; what you would like to give your energy to, and then being fully present to the 'is-ness' of those things as you notice them. You are choosing to recognize a positive aspect of the Now.

The purpose of Active Recognition is to consciously acknowledge yourself or another in times when nothing is going wrong. They give endless opportunities for positive recognitions – after all, even if you are sitting still or having the worst day of your life, you can create this positive self-narration. The only rule is that you should not use it to acknowledge anything negative. Remember Baby Steps: see, with your heart, anything that is not negative as a positive.

These moments are a great way to transform the ordinary into internal messages about your own value. You're taking everyday moments to the 'editing room' and bringing them forth in a way that creates meaning and value for both the giver and recipient of the recognition. You are beginning to create an internal narrative of noticing and appreciating everyday actions and feelings. As these recognitions land in our hearts, we feel profoundly seen, noticed and appreciated. Our energetic sensibilities experience them as successes.

This begins to shift the pattern of needing negativity to create connected relationship. The target of these recognitions comes to feel increasingly meaningful and valued, especially in the absence of drama and negativity. Ultimately, this kind of profound noticing transmits as love.

# Experiential
# Recognition

This technique expands on Active Recognitions by tacking on recognitions of how you, as reflected by your actions, are appreciated. Experiential Recognitions reflect *qualities of greatness* you already have, and those you wish to cultivate further. Let the judgments flow, but judge only in greatness.

"I'm washing the dishes right now. I'm taking responsibility for keeping my space clean and neat. Being organized and self-respecting are great qualities I consistently live by."

"I had to push to get going this morning, but by getting to work on time, I'm showing respect for my co-workers and the tasks at hand."

"Here I am, at exercise class, taking care of my body in one of the ways I've resolved to this year. Afterward, I'm going to eat a big salad for lunch instead of a burger and fries. I'm showing myself love and keeping myself healthy. My awareness and caring are great qualities I have that I am valuing more each day."

We all have qualities of greatness. They are already in us, there for the taking—for the awakening. In coming into the world as this particular self, you made a promise of sorts: to live out those qualities as fully as possible in this lifetime. How do we fan the flames of greatness in ourselves? How can we intentionally build that blaze?

Actively fostering inner wealth and greatness in ourselves is a way to inspire such a shift in our own minds and hearts, and to create ourselves in the image we choose. It is a way to touch into the sacred core of who we signed up to be in this lifetime: a purposeful manifestation of our unique constellation of qualities of greatness.

Qualities of greatness are integral to your being. They are expressed through what you do and how you relate with others and yourself; but they also emanate directly from your essence. Instead of seeing your positive choices and refusal to go negative as caused by some characteristic – courage, for example – begin to see how any courageous choice you make arises directly from a quality of courageousness that is already in you. You are not generating courage from thin air; you are expressing that aspect of your greatness. In seeing that all you wish to express is already within you, you "own" your magnificence, and you need no longer wish, hope or pray for some quality that might seem out of your reach. If you can want it, you must already possess it, and you can foster and expand it by recognizing and appreciating it as a quality of your greatness that already shows up in your ways, means and actions.

You are not asking the universe to give you more of something you want; you are appreciating the qualities of greatness with which you have already been endowed. And by doing so, greatness progresses in its confident, brimming presence and impact in your world. You are remembering who you really are by fanning the flames of the fire that is already part of you.

Another way of conceiving of this is as a *retuning to greatness.* You're like an orchestra going from being out of tune to being exquisitely in tune. As you practice resetting from worry/misery/ doubt into acknowledgment and ownership of your greatness, it becomes ever more effortless. Eventually, you will be able to invoke that greatness thinking in a heartbeat – on the spot. It may be methodical at first, but we are moving toward a place where it's automatic and always accessible – even mystical. You are, essentially, remembering who you really are; you are seeing who you have always been as a being of greatness.

When we appreciate qualities of greatness in self and in others, we demonstrate respect and gratitude for the miracle that is this universe. We are *making* the best of everything we encounter – which will, ultimately, save us a lot of pain and suffering that can easily arise when we think that we have to leap some abstract, externally imposed 'bar' to be truly happy.

The next chapter is a list of qualities of greatness. At any given moment, you can capture yourself expressing at least one of these qualities. Begin to play around with giving yourself (and others!) Experiential Recognitions where you recognize one or more qualities of greatness in the moment. If a particular quality stands out as one you'd like to have more of, give that one special focus. Find even the faintest glimmer of that quality as it is expressed in your daily life. Also notice how others express it, and know that being able to see it in others means it is growing in you.

Notice, too, that not all of the qualities listed are intrinsically positive. As they are usually used, a few have negative implications, but they can be expressed, seen and shaped in positive ways.

The list we provide in the following chapter is by no means a complete list. It is designed to plant seeds of inspiration. As you deepen into this work, you will almost certainly come up with many more qualities to add to your repertoire, which you will use in ways that reflect your uniqueness and creativity.

# Values/Qualities of Greatness
## Worth Acknowledging
### (a sampling)

Abundance · Acceptance · Accuracy · Activism · Adaptability
Adventurousness · Affection · Agility · Alertness · Altruism
Articulateness · Assertiveness · Attentiveness · Awareness
Audacity · Balance · Benevolence · Boldness · Candor · Clarity
Cleverness · Collaboration · Compassion · Confidence
Connection · Conscientious · Caring · Consideration
Cooperation · Courage · Courtesy · Curiosity · Daring
Dedication · Depth · Determination · Dignity · Discernment
Differentiation · Discretion · Efficiency · Elation · Elegance
Empathy · Endurance · Energy · Expansiveness
Experimentation · Expressiveness · Fairness · Faith · Fearless
Ferocity · Fidelity · Flexibility · Flow · Focus · Forethought
Forgivenes · Friendship · Frugality · Fun · Generosity · Good
judgment · Good manners · Good sportsmanship · Gratitude
Guidance · Harmony · Healing · Heart · Helpful · Honesty
Hope · Humility · Humor · Imagination · Independence
Industry · Inquisitiveness · Intelligence · Insight · Integrity
Intensity · Intuition · Joy · Justice/Being Just · Kindness
Knowledge · Laughter · Leadership · Loving · Loyalty
Mastery · Mindfulness · Observation · Open-mindedness
Openness · Organization · Originality · Passion · Patience
Peaceful · Perceptive · Perseverance · Perspective · Playfulness
Power · Precision · Productiveness · Professionalism
Reason · Receiving · Relaxation · Resilience · Resolve
Respect · Responsibility · Restraint · Reverence
Sacrifice · Security · Self-control · Self-mastery · Sensitivity
Service · Spirituality · Spontaneity · Spunk · Stability
Stealth · Stillness · Strength · Sympathy · Synergy
Teamwork Thoroughness · Thoughtfulness · Thrift · Tolerance

Tranquility · Unflappability · Unity · Uniqueness · Valor Vibrancy · Vigor · Virtue · Vision · Warmth · Warriorship (positive power) · Willingness · Wisdom · Wit · Zeal

## Feelings/Emotional States to Recognize

Acceptance · Agitation · Alarm · Amusement · Anger · Angst Annoyance · Anticipation · Anxiety · Apprehension · Aversion Awe · Bitterness · Boredom · Bewilderment · Betrayal · Calm Cautiousness · Closeness · Comfort · Compassion · Contentment Confidence · Confusion · Courage · Disappointment · Discontent Disgust · Delight · Determination · Distress · Doubt · Emptiness Elation · Euphoria · Embarrassment · Empathy · Enjoyment Enthusiasm · Envy · Ecstasy · Fear · Frustration · Gladness Gratitude · Greed · Grief · Guilt · Happiness · Homesickness Honor · Hope · Horror · Humility · Hurt · Impatience · Indignation Interest · Irritation · Isolation · Joy · Jealousy · Loneliness · Love Modesty · Misunderstood · Rejection · Nervousness · Nostalgia Panic · Patience · Peacefulness · Pride · Rage · Regret · Remorse Resentfulness · Sadness · Satisfaction · Shame · Shyness · Shock Suffering · Surprise · Suspense · Sympathy · Terror · Tiredness Troubled · Trust · Understanding · Vulnerability · Wonder Worry · Yearning · Zest

# Proactive
# Recognition

This strategy builds on the first two techniques to give you tools to proactively recognize how you are *not* behaving badly.

What we aren't doing wrong is a topic that rarely gets much play in our self-talk. But consider the greatness available for recognition in any moment you refuse to give in to your less constructive urges.

In years past, I've seen that I am capable of both subtle and blatant forms of rudeness when I'm irritated or frustrated. Therefore, when I am feeling irritation or frustration and I am *not* being rude to others, this is a victory. A *big victory!* In those moments I am living restraint, power and wisdom. Even if I haven't slipped into that rude persona in a decade, this is still a great truth for me. A better way to put it might be that it is a truth of my greatness.

"Wow, you *didn't* burn down your office building today! You're showing great restraint and respect."

Insanity! At least, it *seems* like insanity to those who don't notice how much fuss we make over even tiny increments of things going wrong. Who does it hurt to point out to yourself that, despite your fantasy of throwing something out your window in a fit of road rage, you're continuing to follow the rules? This serves you in two ways: first, by giving you a chance to acknowledge to yourself your angry impulses; and second, by giving you a chance to shift that energy into a much more constructive course of action – recognizing yourself for your power of restraint, discernment, wisdom, kindness and healthy control as you choose to behave in accordance with your values despite temptations to do otherwise. If you even know that possibility exists, credit yourself for the beauty of choosing to take the high ground – even if you weren't even close to tempted to go into a less positive mode.

As a therapist, I've had tremendous success with children who chronically set fires. I even worked with quite a few children who were recidivist fire-starters – who had not responded to heavy-hitting programs designed to scare the hoo-hah out of such kids. Such programs actually fed the fire, so to speak, of negativity. The key was getting the child's parents to courageously express the deep gratitude they felt for each day their child didn't set a fire. Appreciations were given for other good choices too, so that the child felt successful for reasons aside from his choice to not set things ablaze.

Start somewhere, proactively crafting moments of success. When you begin to adopt this attitude that endless success is there for the taking, you find yourself on the edge of a vast vista of possibility.

"Today, I didn't yell at my toddler when he poured his milk all over the floor on purpose."

"Today, I didn't smoke." You can even acknowledge this if you've never smoked in your life. Even if not smoking is easy for you, that choice can be acknowledged as a healthy decision.

"Today, I didn't eat food that was bad for me."

"In the last 15 minutes, I haven't given energy to worries, misery or doubt, although I was tempted to go there."

You are likely to revert to doing some of the things you're congratulating yourself for *not* doing right now. Ingrained habits can be hard to break. But you will have felt the greatness of accomplishment in the moments where you weren't indulging in those habits. Those moments of deeply cherishing your own power, control and wisdom build an energetic foundation that never goes away. They begin to change your defaults and build a new way of relating to yourself. It happens in increments, acknowledgment by acknowledgment. You are accumulating inner wealth. You are nourishing your great soul.

A realm of greatness is always associated with the choice to *not* do something wrong. It doesn't just happen or fall from the sky. It is a deliberate act. Such an act calls for discernment, refined judgment, conviction and commitment, and those are all great qualities. Remember the barometer of how *not-great* not great is. How not great would it be if someone irked you on the freeway and you chose to expose yourself and others to danger by being reactionary? If you choose to feel your emotions deeply and efficiently and churn that very same energy into a response that doesn't make you vulnerable legally and to harm, you are living out an endless array of qualities of greatness. In that same situation, if you muster the courage to act with integrity and honor and even humor, you are feeding that fire of greatness even more.

You've already done this countless times: done the right thing when you could have made a very different choice. The difference from here forward is that you are empowered to honor yourself for it.

# Creative
# Recognition

With children, the methodology of Creative Recognition is designed to energize the child for collaboration in response to requests. A child who has gotten into a car and is just about to finish putting on his seatbelt can be given lots of positive reinforcement for making that good choice. "I need you to put on your seatbelt," the parent might say, and without an aggressive reversal of the course already being taken, the child can't help but comply. The parent then gives the child total credit for the choice he has just made. "Thanks so much for doing that," the parent might say. "I can see that you care about your safety and that you're willing to follow the rules about seatbelts to help me stay out of trouble. You know if I get pulled over and you're not wearing your seatbelt, I get a big ticket! So...thanks for being so considerate and for making sure you won't get hurt if anything goes wrong while we're driving today."

This technique is usually used to help adults move the most challenging children into a place where successes can be richly acknowledged. A child who might otherwise be wildly oppositional gets to experience the figurative ticker-tape parade that comes with success. Imagine the variations: a child who is opening a door, sitting down to do homework, coming down to dinner, or otherwise doing her usual daily routine can be caught in the act this way and creatively recognized.

I advise adults working with children to make it their mission to watch for even little bits of compliance and collaboration in the right direction, and to make the most of the opportunity by way of great, nourishing appreciation: "Billy, I loved that you listened carefully to my directions. I saw that you put down what you were occupied with and got started immediately, and now, I see you carefully making my request happen. I appreciate that you are doing what I asked so carefully and completely even though you may not have wanted to. That shows the greatness of your respect and thoughtfulness." The creative aspect of this technique is in making requests as clear and as simple as needed to eventually find the opening to compliance; and then, in making the recognition strong enough to establish a new pattern of congruent relationship, where a positive choice receives as much energized response as needed to create the necessary impact to override the old patterning.

One important detail of Creative Recognition is that we eliminate a perceived sense of choice when making requests. We don't ask, in a polite manner, using an opening such as "please..." "would you..." or "can you...". Adults use these words with children because they are polite, and they want to set an example of politeness; the problem with them is that they imply that compliance is optional. Most challenging children will opt to not comply – not because they're bad, but because they are not convinced that they can get the strong connection they need through doing what they are asked. They remain deeply convinced that the most satisfying (read: intense) relationship is obtained by disregarding or defying requests.

I contend that the kind of language that usually begins a polite request muddies the clarity of communication even between adults. I'll take clarity and directness over waffling or weak language any day, no matter whom I'm talking with. Go ahead – tell me what you want or need, and take a stand for it! I so appreciate when adults do this with me. "I need you to..." "Here's what I want you to do..." or "This needs to be taken care of now..." works a lot better for me than "would you please...? Can you...?" Think about this for a moment and see whether it's true for you too.

Now, let's consider how this form of recognition – this fourth technique designed to uphold the Second Stand – applies to the greatness practice. You can't really 'trick' yourself into compliance the way you can strategically inspire a child.

We often make requests of ourselves. In our own internal lives, we take on tasks and actions that can be daunting. And often, we fulfill our requests of ourselves in response to some form of internal urging. That self-talk may not be audible to us until we start to pay attention, but for the time being, let's assume that all of us, at some level, have an inner voice that makes requests of us, and that it takes one tone or another to persuade us to act.

The self-talk you are learning to use in this book is designed to create an atmosphere of greatness and inner wealth within you, which then can emanate out into all your relationships in the ways you talk to others. In the greatness practice, Creative Recognition is about making these internal requests in a manner more likely to get a stronger response – and about remembering to see the beauty in the actions we take to accomplish what is needed.

I've experimented with making these inner requests as clear and simple as possible. I use them to command the direction that my highest self – the one who wants to live in and celebrate greatness – wants things to go. I can generate a request for myself, using commanding language. I can then call upon that request when I know I need to guide myself back toward greatness.

Here's an example. I recently noticed that my inner process sometimes hits warp speed to meet the demands of my life. My mind races and I get amped up, making it hard for me to notice when situations call for a slower pace and to adjust my energy to go with that new flow. When I noticed myself overshooting the pace of my current situation, I began to think to myself, intentionally, in *command* form, "Listen up. Be calm," as though I were talking to the cells of my body – as though I were making a direct, firm request to a child. It could have just as easily been, "Here's what I need you to do" or even "Hubba hubba" as long as it did the trick.

As I used this particular inner command, I found that it worked like a charm: everything immediately slowed down. I took it deeper by using my breath to carry this message to every last part of my being, the sacred cellular miracle that comprises me. As I felt myself shifting in response to my own internal command, I made sure to energize myself for the good choices I was making: both the choice to give myself the command, and for my self/ soul's incredible capacity to shift on a figurative dime in response.

Notice where a firm, clear internal request might be useful in your life. Play around with creating internal requests and messaging that help you shift. Make the most of every opportunity to feel and appreciatively nourish any shifts that align with your journey into greatness.

# Amplifying Recognitions with
# Qualities of Greatness

As you work and play with these recognitions, weave in qualities of greatness wherever you can:

"I'm feeling annoyed by this problem at work, but I'm persevering in trying to work it out. Perseverance is a great quality I have."

"Taking this new yoga class is scary for me. Still, I'm going in there to do it, and this bravery is a quality of my greatness."

"I'm mopping the floor, a job I really hate doing. I know it's important to keep my home clean as a way to take care of my family and myself. I am claiming the greatness of caring and concern."

"Although I'm not getting along with my sister right now, I am continuing to try to reach out to her and heal our problems. I'm demonstrating how much I value family and good communication. These are all qualities of my greatness."

"Although I felt like not telling the truth in this situation, I did because honesty is important to me. Being truly honest, and being careful to do so in as sensitive and non-judgmental a way as possible, are qualities of my greatness."

"In giving part of my lunch to the homeless man who hangs out near my work, I showed unselfishness and compassion. This decision reflected these qualities of greatness that I value in myself."

"I'm in a hurry but I'm choosing not to speed on these dangerous roads. How *not great* would it be if I were endangering myself and others? So…how great is it that I am not doing that? My concern for others' safety and the safety of myself is a quality of my greatness."

"When that cashier made a mistake with my items and had to start over, I felt like making a rude remark, but I didn't. Instead, I made a friendly joke and she smiled. My ability to lighten a tense moment is a quality of my greatness."

"When my daughter gave me attitude, I wanted to start screaming at her, but instead I reset myself, gave *her* a reset and then dove in to support her next positive choice. I am the greatness of patience, determination and gentleness."

All of this might seem like a lot of words. But think about how eloquent and long-winded you get when things are going wrong or when you make a choice that you're *not* proud of having made. Those moments bring out the poet in most of us. Channel your eloquence into moments where your choices dovetail with your best intentions. Consider claiming the greatness inherent in these choices. Consider *owning* and *standing* in that greatness. If you elect to 'accuse' others of greatness, I promise you: it will not ruin their day…or yours.

# Googling
# Greatness

Allow me to take you on a quick journey along a secret thread of the truth of your life, where you can manifest and magnify greatness any time you wish.

Imagine that you sit down to log onto the Internet. Much to your delight, you find that your connection is perfect and immediate – the best broadband ever. In the search window, you type your name, along with the word "greatness." Much to your surprise, you find hundreds of results. You scroll down and click on the first one that intrigues you.

When you open it, you are stunned. Your heart begins to pound. Every page is loaded with notes about your particular qualities of greatness. Each paragraph describes amazing, exciting qualities.

For example: One paragraph gives detailed accounts of ways you have been loving. Another talks about your great quality of collaboration. Yet another talks about your greatness in terms of your brilliance and insightfulness. The pages of qualities go on and on.

The entries are dotted with hyperlinks. You double-click on one hyperlinked word, "generosity," and it leads you to pages filled with examples of your expression of this quality. These pages feature precise documentation of multiple episodes where you were generous.

On the 7th of March, 2011, for example, you were standing in line at the supermarket at 4:11 in the afternoon. The man in front of you was impatient at the slowly moving line. You cracked a joke, generously making an effort to bring a smile to his face by using your sense of humor.

This is only one of dozens of bullet-pointed examples evidencing your generosity. The list goes on and on, with even more links to other qualities of greatness. Those links lead you to more pages about linked qualities: your sense of humor, for example, and your kindness. Clicking through, you see long lists of examples of ways you have exhibited humor and kindheartedness.

Following one more link, you find another page that, at first, makes no sense. It seems to document times when you've been told or felt things about yourself that contradicted your greatness. There was that time in middle school when a kid called you names. Another time, one of your parents spoke to you harshly.

Soon, you understand. In each of these instances, had these people seen their own greatness, they never would have said anything that did not support yours. They wanted to support your greatness all along; they just didn't know how. They wanted to connect with you, but at the time, that connection could only come through these more negative interactions.

Reading this is wonderful, but overwhelming. You decide to take a break and try to close the page. But every time you attempt to do so, it springs back open, along with a box that reads:

---

TERMS AND CONDITIONS

To close this page, you need to agree that you cannot now, or ever again, dismiss what you have read today.

You must pledge not to turn your back on what you now know, and you must agree to purposefully fan the flames of these qualities of greatness.

You must agree to return to these pages often; and to purposefully refuse to give your energy to anything that distracts or contradicts this in you.

As soon as you feel an energetic impulse toward distraction from your greatness, you must quickly experience it and then reset yourself to purposefully MAGNIFY GREATNESS—that of YOU and that of OTHERS.

---

You click the box marked "Agree."
There's no turning back.

# The Rivers of
# Yes and No

The *Stands* of the Nurtured Heart Approach represent the confluence of the rivers of "yes" and "no." The more clear you get about the "no," the more clear the "yes" becomes. The more clear you get about what you *don't* want, the more clear you will become about what you *do* want. These clarities meet and amplify one another.

- **Not taking the first stand of refusing to energize negativity undermines positivity, no matter how much you amp up positives.** I've met many who sincerely attempted to be in the space of appreciation and gratitude; and because negativity was still the predominant default setting, nothing shifted significantly. *Stand One creates the space for Stand Two.*
- **If you become less negative but don't fill the space left behind with appreciation, gratitude and greatness, that empty space can and will continue to invite negativity.** This is essentially why "ignoring" not only doesn't work with an intense child or adult, but also will most often make things worse. *Stand Two is at the heart of the shifting default setting to being, living and loving fully in greatness.*
- **If you hold to the first two stands most of the time but don't strictly uphold your commitment to reset when you cross the boundary into negativity, you might temporarily shift your pattern, but a true shift in your default settings is unlikely.** Since we all inevitably take some form of Stand Three – since we all reset eventually every time, anyway – the better we get at resetting *every single time,* sooner than later, the deeper Stand Three goes. In this deepening, the rivers of yes and no lead to the ocean of clarity. Those who master this

process come to a point where they reset right away. As soon as they notice themselves going offline to their greatness, they get right back online – and they become increasingly skilled at noticing as soon as they fall offline. And they become ever more skillful at using the energies of it all to go to ever-better iterations of greatness.

With this in mind, let's look at how these stands might work in a real-life situation. Let's say your boss reprimands you for missing a meeting. Your own story about the situation is that your boss didn't communicate the time of the meeting to you far enough in advance, and by the time you knew about it, you had a conflicting commitment.

Stand One (Absolutely NO!): Refuse to go negative in reaction to the reprimand. Refuse to defend or argue your case, especially in those first moments when you are feeling angry and disrespected. Even if you are flooded with negative thoughts, retorts, or angry statements, and even if you know your stance is justified, uphold the first stand: just don't go there.

Actively listen to your boss' concerns, even if you think he or she is completely off base. Fully feel the emotions driving the urge to react defensively or to say or do negative things. Send all these swirling feelings and thoughts into a powerful reset (Stand Three) that coasts you right into Stand Two. Use the energy of any and all emotions to fuel your next iterations of greatness.

If you don't succeed in this – if you go negative despite efforts to uphold Stand One – recognize that no matter what, you can always choose to start doing so in this next Now. The reset is always there, waiting.

Stand Two (Absolutely YES!): Once reset, energize the positive aspects of the choices you are making. You might say to yourself, "I dealt well with this reprimand. I listened respectfully and did not get defensive because I knew that doing so would cause the problem to grow and might get me fired, and I like my job. I chose to listen and to demonstrate respect and humility.

I am the greatness of discernment, self-control and resiliency." Energize the other person's positive choices and attributes, too, whenever and however you can summon an acknowledgement.

If you need a moment alone to regroup, ask the other person for a brief time-out from the conversation to reset yourself. Arrange a time to continue when you know you'll be calm enough to hold to your stands and energize yourself in greatness. I've even had success saying things like, "I'm going to reset this conversation." This kind of simple, quick request can shift the discussion to a clearer, more purposeful path.

Stand Three (Absolutely CLEAR!): The pathway from problem to resolution in greatness will not always be linear. You may need to reset around the exact same minute aspect of the issue multiple times. You may lose your cool and say or do something you regret. Return again and again to the clarity of Stand Three, which is ultimately about applying the first two Stands as often as necessary and reaching your moments of clarity. Each time around that block, however, will engender greater clarity. The rivers of yes and no and all their contributories really do lead to the ocean of clarity and greatness.

This is partially achieved by deeply feeling the emotions that accompany both negativity and deep appreciation – emotions that can bring up strong levels of fear, worry and doubt. The idea here is to deeply, efficiently feel what is there, on the way to resetting to the present. In so doing, you will receive these emotional messages as inputs about what is true for you. Emotions can be like truth serum. If you turn toward them and fully experience them, they'll provide you with information – vital inputs into the GPS that guides you through your life.

If we are cut off from our emotions, we deprive ourselves of this information feed that can serve to guide us within the sometimes turbulent flow of our lives. If we avoid our feelings, they'll keep trying to surface. They will build in strength. We will need progressively stronger defenses to run from them or bury them.

Feeling deeply and efficiently is a release from this battle. It makes space for us to be grateful for this flow of vital information. It gives us license to lovingly churn it into the fuel that feeds the growing fire of greatness.

Let yourself be curious and light about this. It's more fun to approach this in a spirit of exploration than in a spirit of right vs. wrong. Kicking yourself for slipping into some form of negativity will take you temporarily further offline from the truth of this greatness.

The consequence for 'going offline' is not punitive. It's the video game consequence – the reset back to greatness. You have permission – really, you're encouraged – to slip up, catch yourself, reset, and move into the next iteration of greatness. In trainings, I ask those studying with me to purposefully think of something troubling, and to use the frustration of going offline to inspire next levels of greatness. We don't always have to *find* negativity to churn; negativity does a great job of finding us. Certainly, it will show up on every doorstep, uninvited. The magic happens when we deal with it in this alchemical way. This is my personal practice.

I purposefully walk this talk every day. I do better at it some days than I do in others. Please know that right in the middle of dispensing advice drawn from lofty ideals, I, too, am remembering and forgetting, forgetting and remembering. Resetting.

Growth serum!

# Inspire, Conspire, Expire:
# Greatness Breathing 2.0

You are likely familiar with "inspiration" (inhalation) and "expiration" (exhalation): but in Greatness Breathing, another step lies in between.

**As you breathe in, *inspire:*** allow your breath to imbue your whole being with the qualities of greatness you wish to recognize in this moment, or that you wish to inspire in your life.

**In the moment between inhalation and exhalation, *conspire:*** as the body fills with the precious gift of air and as it reaches the top of your in-breath and before the beginning of the out-breath, be here kNOWing. Conspire in keeping with your growing sense of purpose and your knowing of what you want to do with these moments. To me, conspiring is about taking a warrior stance. It conveys a determined sense of the greatness I want to inspire within myself and, outward to the world.

*Spiritus* is the Latin word for breath. Breath is spirit. Conspire with the greatness of Spirit to be collaboratively purposeful with the energy the breath brings; to conjure and alchemize levels of greatness in conjunction with the qualities being inspired. In those moments, I get excited as I infuse the energy of my breath with the purposeful intention to not only inspire my inner community of cells, tissues and more, but to envision that same greatness-infused energy as it travels out beyond the confines of my being to serve the world. Consider that your journey thus far has given you all you need to explore your own unique ways of making the most of this greatness.

I work with a professional golfer who amazes other golfers with his great power, despite what appears to be a complete momentary pause at the top of his swing. Some breath work modalities hold the breath for a period half the length of the inhalation and exhalation; the pause at the top of each breath is a vehicle for great power as well. Such a momentary pause, in the form of conspiring at the peak of the inhalation, will also support Greatness Breathing's profound gifts of consciousness.

**As you exhale, expire:** see the letting-go of breath as a moment of opportunity. It is a breathing-out of greatness into the world, but at the bottom of the exhalation, you are momentarily without spirit/life force. Every time, this represents a moment of decision: will you be born to spirit again with the next inhalation? Said another way: expiration is literally a death into a next moments of birth to the new you. With each breath, we truly risk not having the gift of another breath. Full consciousness of this fact awakens us to the excitement of yet another opportunity to experience aliveness – to greatness, and to the bounty of YOU.

The more mindfully and lovingly you say "yes" to this, the more you're choosing to live as love and grow in greatness. You are saying "yes" to life, which is an act of love. You are saying "yes" to the exploration of all that is possible.

There is no option to "retire" here – to stop this never-ending cycle/process of breathing in spirit and breathing out spirit. I've long known that if I were to pursue the dream of conventional retirement, I would quickly forget who I am. I would forget my purpose, and would forget to propel my dream: exploring and moving spirit further into full alignment with greatness. I believe that ultimately, this is everyone's dream; it just shows up in infinite variations and levels of realization.

One morning during my own Greatness Breathing practice, I focused on the sensation of breathing *with* my heart. It gave me the sense of not just breath, but of energies entering my heart from all directions. I followed my guidance to "hear with my heart." That gave me the sensation of listening ever more closely to what my heart had to offer. And I followed further guidance to "see with my hearing," which gave me a sense of envisioning what I heard my heart saying.

This served to add precious intention and determination as I got ready to farm the great nutrition of 'everything past'—not just the frustrating stuff, but all the living that has led to this moment. I could feel my experiences being lovingly composted into action through the breath: out into my cells, tissues, muscles, organs, bones, and neurons, all the other aspects of my "first community," my body.

That morning's contemplation was heightened in a curious way: I felt guided to expire that nutrient-rich greatness in a way that felt like I imagine the pulsations of birthing might feel. The term that floated into my mind to describe this was *orgasm of the heart.*

The sensations started and stayed in my heart. It was apparent that I could lovingly and intentionally inspire, conspire and then expire through defined and deliberate contractions that felt like pulsating bursts of energy from my heart. It automatically synchronized with the timing of my heartbeats and propelled my intended greatness out into my world better than ever before. It was as though the generation of these *contractions* was really, in essence, the making of a *contract* pertaining to each determined and intentional claim to greatness—a declaration of sorts.

These orgasms of the heart were not at all sexual. As you hopefully vividly know, orgasms can be a most precious gift of the universe. And as great as that can be, at times I've sensed that there must be further dimension to the experience that I hadn't yet explored—something even more sacred and reverent. Looking back now, more than a year later, I can now say these experiences can come in multiples, multiplying the impact of all the greatness we are igniting.

My play with "conspiring" is a source of incredible joy for me. It has so connected me to living my purpose – the opposite of retirement. I'm sure that if I were to retire, I'd soon be much more *tired,* because I wouldn't be energized by purpose.

Inspire. Conspire. Expire. Be born: bring your purposeful greatness to the world. Die to that greatness and make space for that next sweet breath of life.

# Writing Your Own
# Eulogy, Part 1

I've already shared with you about my challenging, intense mother, and about how most of those who loved her failed to see or acknowledge her greatness while she was alive. I only found a way to see and celebrate her greatness after her passing. This was a big wakeup call. I recognized that if even the most challenging people on the planet can be eulogized in a positive light, it should be possible to honor them in greatness while they are still alive. As you can tell by this point, I'm fascinated with the impact of bringing appreciation and gratitude in this way.

In this spirit, I'd like to lead you through an exercise I often teach in my intensive trainings. Prepare to eulogize the person you are likely to subject to more criticism, judgment and tyranny than any other you will ever encounter: yourself.

Picture, in your mind's eye, Steve Jobs. (I might just as easily have chosen a less controversial figure – Gandhi, perhaps, or Martin Luther King, Jr., – but a more true test, I've found, is to pick someone more controversial.) Steve Jobs has been described as having been extremely contentious and so creatively driven that his personal relationships suffered. He had many propensities and habits that served to alienate people from him despite his brilliance. In the days following his death, however, there was an outpouring of acknowledgements around the greatness of his genius, brilliance, fierce determination, sense of beauty, and creativity, along with many other aspects of his unique constellation of greatness. In fact, many of the qualities celebrated during that time were directly related to the contentious aspects of his nature.

In the sacred space created by the loss of someone's life, we are likely to find ourselves drawn to feel and say all the great things that seem so realized and evident in those precious retrospective moments. Why not honor ourselves and others while we are still alive and well?

Take a minute or so to settle into Greatness Breathing. Inspire, conspire, expire. Then, write a list of ten qualities of your greatness.

Let's say your list reads:

| | |
|---|---|
| 1. Good mother | 6. Creative |
| 2. Good friend | 7. Physically fit |
| 3. Responsible | 8. Curious |
| 4. Passionate | 9. Adventurous |
| 5. Helpful | 10. Fun |

Notice the difference between numbers 1 and 2 and the rest of these qualities. The first two are more general, and it's common for people new to this practice to go to those first. The great thing about this is that these qualities are so easy to "unwrap" – to expand into more detailed descriptions of these qualities. What does it take to be a good mother? What qualities must one have to be a good friend?

A good mother has the greatness of compassion, purpose, loving support, and profound caring. She has amazing intuition, vast protective instincts, and the greatness of a wellspring of heartfelt love. A good friend has the greatness of respect, calm loyalty, and a spirit of fun and play. Good friends possess the greatness of speaking their truth, deep caring, and great-spirited listening.

The other qualities on this list can be unwrapped further as well. Each one can be expanded upon. Mention specific instances where you expressed these qualities of greatness. Use the techniques you've been learning. Play with that for a while, filling out your list. Enjoy the creative flow.

# Writing Your Own
## Eulogy, Part 2

Now: Imagine receiving a call informing you of your own death. Really go there. Hear the voice on the other end of the line.

Instead of being shocked or overwhelmed, you are fascinated. This childlike, open-minded fascination insulates you from any kind of regret, fear or sadness and transports you to a spirited illumination of who you have been as a great person. The seas have parted to reveal the greatness of the life you have lived.

Return to an awareness of your breathing.

Breathe deeply into the person of great love that you are; breathe that out in full acknowledgment. Breathe deeply into the big picture of the person you described in your expanded list; breathe that out in full acknowledgment. See clearly the great choices you have made and the great judgment and discernment you have exercised. Breathe that out as well. *Inspire, conspire, expire.*

You are at a moment of having nothing further to lose. Fearlessness and clarity rise up powerfully within you. You are completely and fully in touch with who you *really* are, at a soul level, and with all that is sacred to your being.

Imagine telling all those in attendance at your memorial service about all the greatness you brought to others and to all your endeavors in your short lifetime. Imagine listening to others testifying to your life, character and impact. If anything other than greatness comes to mind, reset to greatness.

Write it all down. Post it in a place where you'll glance at it often.

# The Warrior
## Path

 A Nurtured Heart moment is one of recognizing and appreciating qualities that directly pertain to the heart of the human soul and human spirit and condition: wisdom, kindness, joy, compassion, intelligence. We see glimmers of goodness as evidence of underlying greatness. We dance into the qualities that realm holds. Doing so consistently will eventually replace – or, at least, become more powerful than – fears, doubts, and worries in our minds and hearts. Greatness becomes the new portfolio of who we really are: our new default setting.

We can choose to dip a toe in the waters of greatness. That might feel like enough. It might feel like an improvement. But there's another option: to adopt a warrior mode.

This entails *relentlessly* accusing ourselves of goodness any time we see even a glimmer of a quality we wish to uphold and enhance in ourselves; *hijacking* ourselves into greatness wherever possible; and *passionately* refusing to miss opportunities to feed those qualities with energy and recognition, pushing and expanding them into ever more greatness.

It's about reflecting greatness with determined power and commitment. This can be done in this moment, no matter what happened in your childhood, last year, 10 minutes, or 10 seconds ago.

A warrior stance means nurturing yourself and others with fierce intention and unswayable purpose. It means taking responsibility for your choices in the moment while also giving yourself credit for all you are doing right in the Now; to committing to de-energizing WMDs as they float in uninvited. Warriorship, in this case, means moving past the old self that sees itself as troubled, as inadequate, as a failure, as unworthy of love: as anything but great. Cultivate a new self-image that is about owning, honoring and polishing greatness. Move into greater greatness all the time.

If you can feel one single spark of greatness in yourself or another, nothing stands in the way of your fanning that flame. Nothing stands in the way of creating a new and brighter flame of greatness that then begins to have a life of its own. You will see ever-more positive repercussions in your relationships and endeavors.

Commitment to this warrior path means you choose the life your higher self envisions. In my own experience, the more warrior-like your intention and expression, the more passionately you go after greatness, and the more the universe starts to kick in its support. You will more quickly and abundantly see evidence that living by, for, and in tribute to greatness *works*.

As you build up steam in a more congruent direction – living into the life you want, instead of battling against the life you don't want – you will see greatness multiply.

Warriorship may bring up associations with war for some, and the warrior may indeed be the best kind of soldier. But holding a warrior attunement has an entirely different intention. It is a level of empowerment that encompasses play, creativity and joy. It's fierce, but it's also light.

I once heard of a medicine man who asked the sick, "When did you stop dancing? When did you stop singing?" To me, this is code for: "When did you stop celebrating the greatness of life and in life?" Dancing and singing are passionate reflections of that celebration, and they can be beautiful vehicles for warriorship, for intensity. Embracing greatness as the blood in the bloodstream of the universe, as sacred life force, keeps us in the flow of celebration, whether or not we are wearing our dance shoes or singing out loud.

# Playing
# Hardball

O ften, when people are first exposed to this way of thinking and interacting, their initial impression is that it's soft and light; that it sugar-coats or avoids the reality that bad things happen and that people do bad things.

Truth is, there's nothing soft about it. It is not a way to sugar-coat or avoid negativity, but an intentional way of transforming it. It is about shifting the way we approach negative thoughts, emotions or actions in a manner that helps us have more of what we want in our lives and relationships. It squarely addresses the way energy and relationship get linked and subsequently stuck.

You are playing hardball when you refuse to forget to acknowledge and reflect greatness, and when you refuse to buy into negativity in yourself or in others. You are playing hardball when your stand of clarity guides you to reset to greatness.

People play hardball all the time around negativity. Some do it by clinging to negative stories and cynical worldviews. Let's admit that clinging to worry, misery and doubt is not the exception, but the rule. Most people focus on problems and the energetic 'hit' they bring. This is shifting, but it's still the predominant default. So many among us are more interested in talking about the problem – in defining it as precisely as possible, pressing themselves and others to comprehend how absolutely unique and difficult was this particular set of circumstances – than they are about transforming their approach to the situation. It is so easy to get lost in and swallowed up by the world of problems. When someone suggests that a positive approach might yield more happiness, more productivity, or better health, they might even cling harder, defending their cynicism and casting themselves as victims in a world where far more is wrong than right. This defense might be anywhere from inadvertent and subtle to fierce and forceful.

We all know people who do this. (In some important ways, it's exactly what I'm doing as I describe the problem of persistent negativity!) And sometimes, they do this artfully, with humor and grace. (Hopefully, that's how I did it here.) I understand that this does have its appeal and its place in the world.

This is not about evangelizing to people who aren't earnestly interested in making this shift, but for those who are, this same "hardball" energy can be applied to shifting those very defaults instead of hanging on to them for dear life. Consider this a personalized invitation to do so, if you are ready.

By playing hardball with the three stands of this approach, we can convert depression, anxiety, worries, miseries and doubts to greatness. Show me your intensity, and I'll show you how it makes you great. If I'm choosing to play hardball, I'm going to see your greatness and reflect it back to you without hesitation – even in the face of negativity or resistance. I will be unapologetic.

If I meet further negativity or resistance, I will unabashedly "notch up" each stand. Notching it up means going deeper into expressing the greatness I see; it means digging further into my commitment to refuse to relate around negativity. It means amping up the clarity of my choice to reset when I get thrown offline into negative reactions. In trusting my heart's expression, I will notch up my appreciation and gratitude.

Part of what's depressing and anxiety-producing in the first place is our having given away our greatness. We've given it away to our superstars, our athletes, our entertainers and our deities. It's time to play hardball in reclaiming what is ours – in reclaiming our greatness. Play hardball. Play big in greatness!

# Wow-
# WE

One day, while waiting for an airplane at the Los Angeles airport, I realized that I *so* wanted people to *see me* – a very familiar mode. The harder I tried to get people to see me, the more people appeared to me to be uninterested and unreceptive. For the first time ever, I experienced the energy of my need as *taking:* as needing something from others to make me whole. The realization was unsettling, but also clarifying and refreshing. In that moment, I saw myself in an energy that was previously an unconscious pattern, and that had left me feeling unfulfilled and insecure. Seeing it was the first step to transforming it.

So: in the flash of that realization, I transformed this to the energy of *giving*. Suddenly, everyone was brilliant and luminescent! The irony was that in the energy of giving, I felt more *seen* than ever before, even in that anonymous space.

Can we switch the flow of the current of being from *taking:* wanting, hoping, seeking, grabbing…to *allowing:* giving, bringing, providing, loving? Every day, the sun rises, showing us all that we can be infinitely giving while asking for nothing in return. The sun is infinitely radiant, even when covered in clouds. It doesn't selectively shine on any one race, place, or identity. Can we hold a similar attunement to an energy of giving? I think we can.

The other irony I see now is that in all the years of taking, of holding the energy of trying to pull people into seeing me, the desperation of wanting to be seen, I felt so drained by my own efforts. In contrast, giving feels renewing and renewable. The funniest thing about all this is that this greatly amplified energy was available with what amounted to the flick of a switch.

This brings us back to the abundance of greatness – the fact that no competition or comparison is necessary. If you or I were the only person alive with the abundance of strength, or love, determination, or any other quality of greatness. It might be like being the only person with a telephone or the only person with an e-mail address. How would that work out? The greatness of both these modes of communication is lost in isolation. Obviously, for all this to fly, we need empowerment for ourselves *and* others.

You wouldn't see yourself as a great boss without seeing the greatness of your employees; a great husband without being a party to the greatness of your wife; a great parent without a grasp of the greatness of your children; or a great teacher without acknowledgement of the greatness in your students. On a globe with limited resources and too many people, competition is a given, but we don't have to fight over greatness. There is no need to make a distinction between your own greatness and the greatness of others. You can broaden, deepen and intensify this practice by referring not only to yourself – "I am greatness of…" – but to the collective *we:* "We are greatness." My personal practice feels at its strongest when I am a party to the "we" that is really the truth of existence. For me, the "wow" is in the "we."

We emphatically do *not* need people to be *less* great so that we can be greater – to the contrary! How not-great would it be to be the only person with greatness? How much fun would that world be? Perhaps about as much fun as trying to swim in an ocean with only one drop of water. Others' greatness only amplifies ours, if we let it. Let's collectively welcome the *wow* in *we.*

# Energetic
# Experiment

My dear friends Susanna and Puran Bair have an adult son named Jered. When I first met them, they had a challenging, sometimes contentious relationship with this young man. I did a role-play with Susanna and Puran where I played the role of Jered and had them talk to me, as him.

I found myself drawn to using my body, without speaking at all, to respond in a pure way to the energy of their statements. When they said something that was truly in the moment and real and positive – "this is what we appreciate about you!" – I allowed that energy to draw me closer. As long as they kept that going, I even let that energy draw me right up onto the table on all fours to get closer to them. I couldn't get close enough. I felt I was able to respond to the energy beneath their words with total honesty.

Like a magnetic force, positive statements drew me in. When the energy started to go critical – and this happened in very subtle ways – I felt myself pushed back. Anything that sounded like advice or a 'pep talk' pushed away. I kept moving away until they went back into statements that were purely grateful and appreciative, without any 'ifs, ands or buts.' This visualization of the impact of their statements helped them gauge where they were leaking negativity in their interactions with Jered, which ultimately helped them navigate a healthier relationship with him over time.

Advice is one way in which attempts to give positive input are actually subtly negative. As we tell the other person what we think he should do, we communicate our lack of faith in his ability to chart his own course (and, when necessary, make his own mistakes). Pep talks and stating of expectations are other common sources of underground negativity. "Come on, I KNOW you can do it!" energetically conveys "...apparently, you *aren't doing it.*"

Following these kinds of exchanges, each person walks away with intensified internal dialogues of worry, misery and doubt.

Try this experiment for yourself sometime. Tune in to the subtle ways in which criticism and nagging emerge, even in seemingly positive communications. You might be surprised at your heart and your body's ability to pick up on and react to negativity that your mind would miss. Those subtle and often inadvertent negative messages are read by the body and the heart more strongly than they are read by the mind. This is why we can be talking to someone who seems to be saying positive things to us, but we have a body sense that makes us want to run in the other direction.

In the same vein, experiment with observing subtleties from others in response to your words as you interact verbally. While you contribute to an interaction, see into the truth of the energy of your words and feel the energy of the impact of the other's words as they arrive in the sphere of your being. Read energy like Braille. The greatness of your beautiful sensitivities will give rise to new layers that will inform your life.

# Clearing the
# Hard Drive

One day, my computer went quirky and slowed down. It said, "Startup disk full." My friend Jim, a computer expert, gave me huge caution to back everything up, post-haste. He'd had the experience of losing years of poetry and other creative work in a full-scale computer crash. I could hear his sadness as he reminisced. I did back everything up, and deleted a lot too, but the disk was back to full within a few days.

With the help of a second or third specialist, I finally figured out the problem: a rapidly multiplying "ghost file" holding backups of a mail folder that contained large files, including a sizeable video from YouTube that someone had sent to me. This was what was taking up all my space. When the Mac expert reset my hard drive to eliminate this ghost, I had my computer back. There was something to be done to create renewed space and buoyancy, and we had done it. The moment my computer released the harmful file, two-thirds of the space on my hard drive was freed up for use and storage.

Is a parallel process possible for us? Might we have rapidly replicating data on our 'hard drives' that takes up all the space? Do our perseverations on certain worries, fears or doubts start creating 'ghost files' that start automatically replicating behind the scenes – replays of replays that consume our available life force? Could this create a kind of energy crisis that would undermine one's intention and purpose, leaving longed-for journeys un-embarked upon or under-energized?

Let's say our own 'hard drives' – our minds – also fill with 'ghosts': all the energetic replications of life we drink in every day, life 'replays' along with all the You Tube videos, all the Facebook and other media feeds. Copy upon copy upon copy they collect, taking up space in our being.

What if we could just take these jumbled fragments and delete them – move them to the Trash bin? Not just negative aspects, but anything, negative or positive…literally everything that is not the Now?

We wouldn't be deleting people, character, or circumstances, but rather just the energetic programming that runs underneath everything and that consumes the space of our being – space that could otherwise be inhabited by growing constellations of greatness. That programming's energy brings an interfering magnetic force that distracts and diminishes the freshness of our pure experience of the moment.

I contend this is the very force that creates system overloads, crashes our senses of harmony, and creates dilemmas of health and happiness. I contend that in resetting this energetic field to greatness by releasing these non-functional fragments, there is a clearing of precious space for us to thrive all the more in greatness. I contend that there's nothing to lose and everything to gain.

# The Snoring
# Epiphany

At the Omega Institute, I participated in a Gabrielle Roth Five Rhythms dance workshop. After three days of dancing for hours a day, I was exhausted. But in the dorm, someone was snoring at a volume that totally ruled out my falling asleep. It was in the next room, but this person may as well have been sleeping next to me, snuffling and snorting directly into my ear.

To the credit of the Institute, they had warned that the dorms could present just such a difficulty and had advised attendees to bring noise-reducing gear. I had a noise-reducing machine and noise-blocking headphones, and I set myself up to try to get some rest. But the level of the snoring in the next room was so ear-splitting that, even with all this paraphernalia turned all the way up to 'thunderstorm' setting, I wondered if I might somehow actually be inside this person's nose.

So there I was, in this world-renowned center for personal growth, ready to commit murder or suicide out of exhausted frustration. As I fully experienced the next Now, I saw that I was doing a worry-doubt-fear voiceover, fully immersed in my WMD software.

RESET!

I made a choice to flip the switch to splendor and greatness. I got back online and turned toward an active state of participation and collaboration with the unfolding Now in the context of greatness. In this new moment, lying in my bed next door to the King of Snorers, as producer, director and editor of the next frames, I chose to intercede from a place of greatness.

I began by breathing greatness as deeply as possible, while also experiencing the reality as deeply as possible. Those realities included my inner state of fear of not sleeping; doubting and worrying whether I could function in the workshop after a sleepless night; and my anger toward the snorer. From there, I brought an additional condition to the editing room – imbuing each and every frame with a mindset of greatness. This meant using the energy of each bit of doubt, worry, fear and anger to further propel the trajectory of that instilling process, going deeply, steeply into greatness through the magic of that powerful energy.

And next thing I knew, it was morning. Somehow, miraculously, I had fallen asleep despite the rattling walls. Better yet, the journey that night into greatness was still with me when the sun came up. I awakened pre-set to a day of greatness. And thus it was.

Sometimes it feels that the toughest moments have the greatest potential yields. I have been around for a few births, and I know I'd be on thin ice if I said this must be what it feels like – so I won't say that. I'll say that some of these most painful moments are there to tell us that a new download is ready to be delivered and needs a cosmic push of sorts. I'm sure many laboring women have used the extra energy of fear, worry, doubt and anger to provide just that extra push that finally birthed a great gift into the world.

The reset is a highly efficient variation on meditation. It allows us to regain balance and find a peaceful, positive, connected place right in the raging river of everyday life. It can happen in a flash: feel the angst quickly, vividly and efficiently, then let it go and move on to yet more greatness.

# Applied
# Greatness Breathing

Have you experimented with Greatness Breathing yet? Let's revisit and expand on it, because the breath and the body are important parts of this practice. You can do it in your head, but that's not where your heart lives, and it isn't all of who you are. Why not allow every part of yourself to participate in this journey?

Between inspiration and expiration, we have the choice always to *conspire*. Within each breath comes a moment where we truly decide who we are; what we are going to do with who we are; and what we are going to do next in support of who we are…where we purpose and repurpose our intentions and initiatives. To what extent will we consciously conspire to live our greatness and our great purpose?

For at least 15 years, I have used my mind, heart and breath to hold the phrase "The Nurtured Heart Approach is spreading far and wide" in my awareness. I do so with focused intention and great purpose. With the sweet inbreath, I conspire to make that vision real, and with the sweet outbreath, I send it out into the world. Please know that I'm not breathing this intention as a tool of marketing, but rather because of my sense of my purpose and life's work.

What I have planted now has a life of its own, even though I have done this for less than one minute per day at most. As I circulate that vision throughout my own body and send it out, it grows like a lovingly tended garden. Even when parts of the garden are rerouted, pruned, weeded or cut back, new shoots keep coming, and its bounty is abundant.

The complete outbreath enables me to trust that the gifts of greatness that I have acquired and that I continue to nourish in this way can be released: sent out fully on the outbreath. As I refill/refresh myself through the inbreath, I 'refresh my browser' to the next Now.

Exhaling is a letting-go. Consciously expelling all the stale air in the lungs can bring up discomfort, even fear. Exhaling is the last thing we will do in our brief time on this planet. Trust that, until then, each time you trust that a full exhalation will be followed by a new, fresh inhalation, you are trusting the sacred nature of Now.

Can I practice expiration to the point that I get truly comfortable with 'dying' – letting things go – "not knowing?" The reward: staying much more open to what can happen in the moments to follow – the beauty of being awake. In our society we are so accustomed to holding on and wanting things to be the same. Instead of dreading change and striving to stay the same, can we stay present now and enjoy wherever the next moment takes us? The breath is such a useful reminder to do this. Use it.

Try this: Take a deep inbreath and tell yourself, "I am the greatness of the universe." On the outbreath, tell yourself, "we are the greatness of the universe." Feel your heart as the transmitter of that love. Let the breath come from the heart, with the exhalation moving love out at 360 degrees all around the heart.

The question this continually begs for me, and which never ceases to bring the joy of exploration, is: To what level can I conspire next?

# I Am
# Appreciating

A few years back, at a week-long advanced training for the Nurtured Heart Approach, I was chatting with my fellow facilitators as breakout groups were finishing up. The participants' assignment was to take turns appreciating one another. In the background of our chat, many people in different small groups were saying "I am appreciative of [something in that other person.]" However, from my perch in the distance, all I could hear was a humming, continual "I am."

"I am" sounded distinctly like a chant of "Om," the Sanskrit word often intoned in yoga and other spiritual practices (which also happens to mean "I am"). In the blur of it all, I had an epiphany: that appreciation is the sound of the universe. Once I had made that connection, "I am" became the sound of appreciation in action: gratitude, love of being, and acknowledgment of the greatness in self and others.

I love the feeling of ending participation in a yoga class with a moment of sweet reverence: an expression of honoring the practice, the teacher, my fellow students, and myself. Most often a Hindustani word, *namaste* (pronounced *nahm-as-TAY*), is used to reflect this honoring. My translation of this word is: "The greatness in me sees the greatness in you."

Often I wind up taking classes at the end of a busy day, and it is a beautiful way to bring the day toward culmination with a focus of sweetness and appreciation. Taking a class first thing in the morning sets a tone for the day: to see and honor the greatness in self and others.

One day where I attended a morning class, I remembered how, for so many years as a youth on the run – running from my intensity, my emotions, and the life of greatness I clearly had within me – I had, in effect, unconsciously, set up the intention of every next day being yet another "numb-ass day" – a day of not feeling, a day of negativity, and a day of navigating my world through a whirlwind of ineffectual activity.

It felt sweet to realize that by living my passion and by honoring my intensity and emotions I can, in contrast, have and hold the intention of yet another "namaste"— and to truly know that this is fully a function of my manifestation. The greatness in me sees the greatness in you. Namaste.

# Welcoming the
# Blessing of Change

I love the game of golf. It gives me abundant opportunities to stay in the Now. No matter how well I hit the ball on the driving range today; no matter how clearly I think I now know just how to replicate that beautiful shot; and even if I have total recall of that the next day and I get out there and feel like I am swinging in precisely the same way, it is never, ever the same.

This used to frustrate me, but I've learned to welcome and embrace the exploration it encourages. This letting-go, this welcoming of change, has increasingly allowed me to adjust faster in life, to complain less, and to move forward in ways I would have never guessed possible. I have heard it said that the only thing that stays the same is change; but until I experienced the beauty of this from the inside out I still fought it, hanging on to past moments and trying to drag them into my current experience. As I relax into the Now, all the previous iterations of my swing come together effortlessly, allowing me to adjust readily to what's next – either through my own discovery or by way of a teacher's sharing.

Try this as a practice. Hold the statement "I am the greatness of wisdom" in your mind. Inspire it into your body, then conspire it out through you to the extent of your imagination. Lastly, breathe it through all your cells and systems and on out into the world, fully releasing it.

Understand this expiration as an ending to the last iteration of life and simultaneously a welcoming to the next; a 'death' to what was and a red carpet to what is. Trust that you can expire with each breath and still be there essentially as *you,* welcoming the sense of being and the change that is inevitably woven into the texture of your universe...of *our* universe.

Trust that you can 'go offline' for that brief moment, and that when you return, when you recognize swiftly and efficiently that you are offline and that you want to get online again, you can inspire, conspire, and expire a new and expanded version of you and the next delicious version of Now.

# Oceans
## of Clarity

Now let's return to the Third Stand: absolute clarity about where you want to put your energy, purpose and luminosity, and dedication to living life from that clarity. To me, this stand is about our relentless intention to be in greatness – our growing clarity about claiming our unique, beautiful personal constellation of great attributes. This is the stand of owning and living the highest version of who we really are. This stand is the *refusal* to not be in that clarity.

This means staying resolute. Even though the only constant in life is change, you can continue to stay present, alive and dedicated to the beauty of being your greatness. You can remain dedicated to resetting once you notice yourself falling offline. It doesn't at all mean not having strong feelings. Issues and negativity will most likely arise. It *does* mean fiercely realizing when we get offline to that greatness, and it means acting with bold determination to get back online.

Progressively get clearer that any degree of 'camping out' in negativity takes you away from the joy of being online to who you really are. Get progressively clearer that negativity will not produce benefits like gratifying and sympathetic relationship with self or others. With the same level of clarity, keep returning to the view that any shred of negativity serves best an impetus to get to a higher trajectory of all that is great – as fuel for the fire that is you.

Getting clear about the line is an art. A few important parts of this process include:

- Letting intuition speak
- Feeling into the body's wisdom

- Creating space for knowing
- Lovingly resetting as needed
- Accepting that emotional fallout will accompany at least some resets
- Enjoying the ever-changing view of greatness from ever-new vistas – not holding on to what was
- Welcoming next levels of clarity

Make conscious choices about what to do with any fallout. Decide how to manage that energy congruently with your intentions, and then compost it back into greatness, progressively enriching the primal nutrition of your being.

It's magical to be around people who have clarity around their choices: what they want in their lives, what their personal boundaries are, and what sustains, motivates, and inspires them.

One contributory to the glory of the ocean of clarity is what we *don't want* in our lives – Stand One. This First Stand always adds momentum, flow and impact as it fosters sweet clarity about the *NOs* in our lives. Become increasingly clear about what *doesn't* sustain you, what *doesn't* motivate and inspire you, and what brings you to adverse feelings and reactions.

The other great contributory to the glory of the ocean of clarity is what we *do want* in our lives – Stand Two. The "yes" of Second Stand gets sweeter and ever-more clear as we become progressively grateful and *great-filled* through choosing to be expansively appreciative of all that is and the greatness inherent in our navigation of life.

This ocean of clarity is an ocean you can swim in. It's an ocean you can rejoice in; the ocean of you.

# All
# In

In my childhood, my reactive mantra was, "Leave me alone." I would say this to myself often, and would also share it freely out loud many times a day, with varying degrees of ferocity. I perceived adults as unsupportive and persistently demanding ("in my grill," as I have described it to friends). I threw away many gifts of opportunity throughout the ensuing years, because at some level, I held on to that mode. I had somehow decided I was "all out" and this led me to hold back, protect my energy, and retreat from life.

This finally shifted for me at a Yoga, Purpose and Action Leadership Intensive with Seane Corn, Hala Khouri, and Suzanne Sterling. In the context of this workshop's physical yoga practices, I saw how I was still holding on to that mantra of "leave me alone," and I grasped how much it had gotten in the way. Those issues had taken hold deep in my tissues, as Seane would say, but they had started to move under the brilliant guidance of Seane and her team. By the time I left the week-long training, I had intuited a new mantra: "I am all in."

Around the same time, I experienced, for lack of a better term, my first "rock star" weekend. It wasn't really real rock-star caliber, but in one weekend, I attended a gala fundraising event where I got dressed up with the Tucson arts crowd; then, I had to leave for a before-sunrise flight to LA, where I gave a presentation in the morning; and I came home the same day so that I could attend another evening event and yet another event the next day. It all felt larger-than-life and purposeful. I was giving my all and having fun along the way.

As I joyfully gave myself to the flow of life and enjoyed the ride, I felt like I was living the new mantra: *I'm all in* – or was it living me? Either way, I was embracing it all: the fullness, the excitement and vitality, the exhaustion and gratification, all of it full-tilt and exciting. The mantra, which at its core is simply *energy* to live by, had come to life. "I'm all in." I had more energy and felt more fluidly congruent with my heart's desires.

Even then, I sensed a next iteration on the horizon – yet another trajectory of this ever-expanding energy. I lived my way into it two years after launching "I'm all in." I attended a second leadership workshop, again with Seane Corn and the Off the Mat, Into the World team. As I participated, another refinement floated in – in the form of my next mantra, which immediately began sparking more splendor into form: "Playing BIG in greatness." Since then, another two years have passed, and I've been watching this percolate. More greatness.

I invite you to intuitively source and continually renew and upgrade your own mantra of greatness. My guess is that one is already there, waiting to emerge in alignment with a pervasive motto, theme, or themes. If you already have mantras or affirmations, consider resetting them to new versions that are more energetically aligned to your latest vision of your purposeful, great self. If your mantra is already great, the challenge is to make it greater yet. And then, fasten your seat belt, because it will find its way to beautiful manifestations in your life.

# Post-script:

As I review and polish this chapter, I'm spending time in the great city of Sacramento. I've just realized a need for some icing on the cake of "Playing BIG in greatness." I'm choosing to tweak and polish my mantra on the fly.

Let me share my thinking. "Playing" in greatness has been wonderful, but there's a nagging little fly in the ointment that my intuition has picked up on. Many great possible new initiatives related to my Nurtured Heart work are coming my way. These possibilities do feel playfully delightful, and now it's time to take it one more step. I want the playfully delightful possibilities to *land*. It's manifestation time.

I'm just letting myself experiment and feel into the depth, breadth, clarity, intention and beauty of whatever I choose to invest my energy in. I don't want to 'waste my breath,' so to speak; rather, I wish to be a party to making things happen. So, I'm just letting my heart speak as I explore and play transparently in mantra-making.

"Manifesting BIG in greatness."

or, simpler still, "Manifesting magnificence"…

or "Magnificently manifesting collaborative greatness."

Yes, this is playful, but I recognize the importance of exactitude here in concert with readiness for next steps into action. Different words hold different resonances and unlock different frequencies and different doors. Words hold power to move mountains and to make things happen…to make projects land.

I still haven't settled on my new mantra, but I will keep you posted. And I encourage you to play along with your own mountain-moving mantras.

# Compounding
# Greatness

What kinds of complex greatness can you explore or invent?

Take a quality of greatness like kindness or brilliance; then, use modifying adjectives to create a more polished harmonic with deeper nuances and more precise articulation. Create a combination of words that amplifies and reverberates at the heart level, in alignment with your unique sense of resonance. Find and breathe a vibrational vector to explore the depth and breadth, height and width of your growing edges of greatness. Relish the exploration of all that is possible, playful and fulfilling.

Thoughtful generosity

Inspired benevolence

Far-reaching curiosity

Unflappable courage

Buoyant playfulness

Refined integrity

Pristine resolve

Relentless positivity

Fearless clarity

Fierce tenacity

Graceful dignity

Inspired vision

Dignified grace and honor

Perceptive thoughtfulness

Rambunctiously playful

Unapologetic audacity

Greatness-filled expression

The possibilities are truly endless...

# Full-Time Inner
# Congruence

My friend Ben pointed out to me that some people only take great care of themselves when they are sick. The sick person may adjust his or her diet, rest, and self-nurture until the sickness passes, and then may go right back to poor habits once well.

As Ben described his observation of this phenomenon, I saw it as yet another common way we can so subtly and inadvertently find our way to creating profound connection through angst. Conversely, an illness can raise the bar of self-care going forward. We can use that reminder of the greatness that is physical health to improve our self-care habits to a new level. We can take great care of body, mind and spirit all the time.

It is unusual to find a person who wants to maintain connection pervasively and thoroughly through positivity and drama-free living, even though I believe we'd all like to think we could. I've known many people who didn't trust that they could sustain the initial connection they felt with me – a connection they liked and wanted to maintain – by continuing positive aspects of conversation, discussion, and appreciation, or by talking about new, positive experiences. Instead, they reverted to modes of being contrary, antagonistic, problematic, complaining, or deprecating, seemingly in an effort to maintain strong connection. As they slipped into this mode, they did not seem to mind – or even notice – that this connection was forged through negativity.

This is a default in our culture, so this is no big surprise when it happens; still, I am increasingly not willing to go there. If it is a person I want to maintain relationship with, I will sometimes offer up a reset to re-route the connection back in a positive direction or transparently, kindly offer my truth. Sometimes this works.

When it doesn't, I do not tend to want to keep showing up in the relationship.

I can look back at my past, pre-Nurtured Heart Approach, and know that there was loss of relationship when significant others decided to no longer put any energy into connection with me because I had slipped into a negative state. Although I didn't know it at the time, this was the medicine I needed to fuel next iterations of greatness that would give me a better shot as sustaining positive relationship next time around the block. Dissolutions of marriages carry this same healing potential. We may wish it didn't have to be such drastic medicine; but often, that is what is required.

Maybe the first true marriage anyone has is to oneself. Can we, even in the most challenging times, really be there for ourselves – not throw ourselves under the bus? Can you imagine making this same choice: to gently refuse to create inner connection through negativity? To take exquisite care of ourselves all the time, not just when we are sick; and to choose to relate in positivity or not at all?

Remaining conscious and clear in our stands allows us to see ourselves slipping into negativity, and to be so healthy in our 'online' sense of greatness that we refuse to go offline. Can we use all our temptations to go there – all the energy of the worry, misery and doubt – and heartfully reset that energy to greatness? This is what I have been striving for over the past few years, and despite challenges that have become yet more fuel for the fire, I can dutifully report: so far, so great.

# The Delicate Art of
# Resetting Others

A woman conveyed to me via e-mail that when she'd heard me speak in public sometime during the previous year, she had found it deeply disappointing. I wasn't living my approach, she said, and this was because she had seen me reset someone in public. Her perspective was that this was demeaning to the person who I had reset.

Demeaning others is definitely not a feature of the Nurtured Heart Approach, nor would it ever be my intention. It wasn't anything anyone else seemed to notice, so I knew there must be something she either didn't quite understand or that I needed to convey better.

At first, I was a little hurt by what she said, as I have been in other instances where I am told I'm not living my approach. Walking the talk of my approach is hugely important to me. So, I strove to clarify to her my reasons for resetting participants right within the flow of my trainings and lectures.

I explained that most of the time, when I reset someone at a training, it is because he or she has veered the group away from a pathway of understanding to which I'm attempting to lead participants. I welcome interaction that is "on point" with that conveyance. If someone takes the conversation in a direction that undermines the learning curve of the entire group, I offer the reset as a gentle way to bring us all back on track. In a larger sense, I am resetting the conversation to stay within its focus and purpose. I also freely express my deep appreciation for all efforts to get the discussion back online.

Despite my attempt to convince her that the reset I gave was in total keeping with the spirit and letter of the Nurtured Heart Approach, this person remained disillusioned by my choice to reset a participant. She was determined to stay focused on the perceived hurt she saw in the reset, and stuck with her story about it being counter to my method. That's okay. This woman's 'accusation' gave me a great opportunity to clarify why resetting is, in fact, an act of kindness – a most generous thing one person can do for one's self or another.

When a friend or colleague says to me, "Reset, Howie," I always feel appreciation, even if some part of me is resistant and wanting to go down that well-worn road to WMDs. This simple lightning bolt of clarity almost always sets the conversation back to looking at either the positive and purposeful side of things or at what needs to happen to get to what is important or pressing.

I get how, at first hearing, the reset can seem disrespectful or dismissive between adults who are supposed to be on an equal footing in terms of authority. Ultimately, though, the self-reset and the reset of another person are founded in the same principles of awakening greatness discussed in this book, when used with sensitivity and positivity. Resetting another person is no different than resetting yourself when it is done with the intentions of kindness and igniting greatness.

When the occasion to reset another person arises, it is also a gift of energy that makes next levels of greatness available. People who seem to stand in your way as you shift into seeing and being greatness are often the greatest gifts; they remind you to uphold your Third Stand of absolute clarity, even if this requires the making of difficult choices. Sometimes it takes a challenging or contentious person to push you to that next great level of clarity.

You might lose your bearings and pour yourself into negativity in an attempt to transform the other person into someone who doesn't challenge you quite so much, but in the end, it will always boil down to your choices in each engagement, each exchange. Any exchange where another wishes to go negative or in a direction that otherwise doesn't work for you is not cause for argument, attack or defense, but rather for an un-energized and clear reset, either for yourself or the other person, or (more commonly) for both.

Besides: even the most insurmountably toxic person can serve as a reminder that greatness is everywhere. Even the person who infuriates you at every turn has greatness buried in their hardware, in their core. Holding this in your awareness can make a huge difference to you in relation to the person, even if that person never budges a centimeter toward who she really is.

In the extreme, as you move into this, you will find that some people are just flat-out opposed – even contradictory – to this practice. The contradictory person or situation is not necessarily bad by nature; it's just a matter of how he or it draws people in at this moment in time: through negativity. This is that person's current software program. No new downloads are in sight. The person is, for the time being, offline to who he or she really is – a person with inherent greatness.

Some people are stuck in adversity because it has been their way of navigating the world and relationships. Many are convinced that there's much to be gained with that approach. In our world, a negative approach to drawing people in can work well, on the surface. Once this way of connecting with others is established, it may be scary for them to try something new. Even entire organizations can be stuck in a dynamic of negativity. We may all have known at least one such person or organization, and their pull can feel irresistible.

We may be stuck in a relationship with such an individual through family or work, and their presence in our lives may feel like a burr in the side of our movement into positivity – into seeing and growing greatness. While you may see such a person's great qualities, you may find yourself repeatedly drawn into his or her drama, to your own detriment.

With a person like this, you can empathize. You can try your hardest not to energize negativity. Still, when a person has the deepest relationship with himself when he is steeped in negativity, it may be a lost cause. This depth of relationship may be central to who he feels he is. Letting go of it would be threatening to his sense of self. If you fail to play into this paradigm, you may bear the brunt of that person's displeasure and criticism. This kind of person may have intense inner self-relationship when complaining, raging, and judging. They may argue vehemently in favor of an approach to life that is steeped in worry, envy, fear, competitiveness, blame, shame, anger or other negative emotions.

You needn't change anyone else, and you needn't lose yourself around someone else's gravitational pull. Just keep firing up your own blaze of greatness. Continually reset yourself to even greater greatness every time you encounter your frustration with this person, group or organization. This last choice actually 'converts' the energy of frustration to propel a warrior-like stance and trajectory. Send spirited blessings to those who bring the contradictory energy of negativity.

Even if this person or situation remains impervious to your efforts, you and everyone else you encounter will benefit from this higher trajectory and greater determination to see and be *your* greatness. You may even look back and feel indebted to this adverse person or situation. They simply called you to a new level of seeing and being in greatness.

If you do not or cannot choose to walk away from such a person, keep in mind that he can have his angst, and you can bless him in it. Let the relationship be about resetting to joy and gratitude or choosing to silently revere the greatness you know to underlie the current situation. You can see it; that person, for whatever reason, can't, at least not right now. He might get his cosmic jolt from anguish and WMDs, and that is what he will want to talk about...but you can gently, lovingly *refuse* to have that conversation. Instead, point out how great he is and refuse to have relationship with his problems. Use your angst to "notch up" both your refusal and your next rounds of recognition. Steadfastly give love, energy and relationship when negativity is absent. This will serve to create stronger relationship when angst is not happening.

I have fallen in love recently with the expression "save your soul." Save your soul for moments free of problems. Give the energy of your soul as fully as you wish in terms of gratitude or greatness or whatever feels right. Refuse to give the precious gift of your soul's energy in response to the quagmire of negativity.

# On
# Transparency

New learners of the Nurtured Heart Approach sometimes rankle at what seems like a less-than-truthful way of reflecting reality. The Three Stands don't preclude truth-telling, however; we simply tell the truth through a lens of refusing to energize the negative and of giving our energy to what is positive. The Nurtured Heart Approach is about positivity, but it is also about being straight up – telling the truth, in kindness.

Let's say I say this to someone: "You looked frustrated by what I said. I appreciate that you didn't get reactive. You could have yelled and melted down, but instead, I saw you take a breath and consider your options. I appreciate that so much." This is what I choose to see and describe. This is truth. This is transparency.

To illustrate this further, let's turn to a topic that often challenges truth-telling: romance. How many times have you been in a situation with a beloved (or prospective beloved) where you wanted to say something challenging, but couldn't get the words out? Or you said it and it didn't go well? What if there were a way into difficult conversations that brought it all back to greatness – even when the outcome doesn't involve staying together? In sharing my own stories of transparency in romantic relationship, I hope to show you that this is possible.

*I Can Do* Now: After a few dates, Rebecca asked, "Is this a lark or a relationship?" I asked for some time to hang out with this question, and went 'online' to see where contemplating the *greatness* of this situation would lead me. After a short time, I felt a spark in my radiance and resonance. I realized that I didn't know the truth of the future, and it was hurting me to even begin to try to inhabit thoughts that removed me from the present moment. So I shared that truth: that I didn't know what the future held, but in the moment, I wanted to remain fully in the present with her, appreciating her and all we were sharing.

A bit down the road, once it was established we were not building a future in our connection, we kindly, calmly decided to not remove ourselves from the NOW with plans, promises or judgments. Complete transparency allowed us to both walk away feeling contented and finished with what was a delightful time together.

I am not advocating intimate connection without commitment. What I am in favor of is transparency and sensitivity to one's own feelings and expectations in each moment of any relationship, whether new or old, temporary or eternal; and holding the space of greatness throughout, resetting whenever necessary. Commitment can align beautifully with being present to the truth of the moment. They are not mutually exclusive; rather, they enhance one another.

Imagine entering into a relationship while in this heartful, transparent, present space I've described. How much difficulty could we avoid by lovingly saying "no thanks" to plans for the future without denigrating the present? How about just being with another person while saying no to the WMDs that will predictably roll in, and just staying in the space of the Now and greatness? If we can do that, it's easy to judge when we want to continue to have next Nows that include this person. These are the beginnings of conscious relationship.

A conscious relationship has to include *differentiation,* which is the ability to stay true to yourself when in close relationship with the actions and thoughts and feelings of others. When you are able to differentiate, you can rest securely inside yourself without being swept away by other people's emotions, opinions or moods. By way of the greatness of differentiation, you can have an openness that WMDs prohibit. Differentiation is a great quality that encompasses other qualities of greatness: clarity, discernment, thoughtfulness, decisiveness, resolution, giving and receiving, truthfulness, intuition, knowing, openness to change, sensitivity to others, trust, and so much more.

We are given endless opportunities to move from stuck places to unencumbered, exciting versions of being great in the present moment. The way there always involves transparency: truth-telling from a place of love. Conscious relationships are an amazing way to move through issues that would otherwise be difficult to access. Consciously relating in appreciation and transparency will always be wonderfully surprising to me; growing up, I never thought this was even remotely possible. Whenever quagmires and crossed wires lead to negativity in relationship, practice seeing it as the perfect gift of the universe: opportunities to heal old wounds in the company of another.

*Oh Maybelline:* Once upon a time I was in love and in over my head. Maybelline was, to my eyes, stunningly beautiful; and most of the time, she was loving and positive. After a summer of romance, she accepted a job that took her thousands of miles away. When I went to visit her, an unfortunate dynamic I had noticed before emerged full-force.

On occasion, Maybelline had an enigmatic way of misinterpreting my communications. Even saying something incidental and innocuous was sometimes enough to provoke a reactive barrage from her. In those moods, she seemed unable to hear me for what I intended. If I was quiet – which I became more and more, because I didn't want to amplify the situation – she accused me of being angry. Any explanation could create an avalanche of new issues. She expressed repeatedly that she wanted me there with her, but as the visit went on, I came to feel hurt, raw and betrayed: cast as the bad guy. Since we were in a remote spot (unbelievably remote), I didn't have the choice to up and leave. There was nowhere else for me to stay, and planes left the island once a day on most days, but not all days…travel conditions permitting.

An amazing opportunity began to appear: to see a place in my life where I had a major software glitch; where in the past, I had come to believe that I was crazy, wrong and guilty, and that everything was my fault. The gift of this relationship was that it was bringing me back into that space.

I saw that this was a perfect opportunity to strengthen my core being and belief in myself at a level that would bridge and heal this gap. I didn't have to go off and worry my wounds; I could stay right where I was and use this opportunity to build my inner wealth and strength to where I could stop groveling or relinquishing myself, and where I would be able to walk away without anger but in dignity and confidence, knowing I had learned what Maybelline had showed up to teach me. Once I learned that lesson, I would no longer need to be connected to anyone in this way. I didn't need to convince Maybelline that she was wrong, or that I was, in fact, a good guy. I couldn't be transparent with Maybelline about this realization; nothing would come of it. She wasn't available for that level of relating. *My best option was to be transparent with myself* about what was going on, accept my part in it – and grow my greatness in the process of walking away.

The day I decided to try to leave the island, no flight went out because of bad weather. I went back to stay one more night, resolving to hold on to my new little handhold of freedom. Honoring myself, I reminded myself that she was simply stuck. I could forgive and honor her while remaining in love and in greatness rather than in unloving insanity.

It wasn't easy to stay in greatness. My wounds were strong and fresh, and my attention kept going back to them. I reset myself and consciously brought myself to new thoughts of greatness, over and over again. I realized I could make that choice in each moment, no matter who I was with. Doubts came and went; I fell off the horse of awareness and got back on. I was propelled to vastly deepen my sense of inner wealth. When it came time for me to leave, Maybelline told me she wished I could stay. Wishing her only the best, I left.

Living in greatness helps keep people who live in negativity at a distance. When we refuse to tangle with them in that negativity, they lose interest, fast. Resist any temptation to teach or change the other person. Heal the energetic side of the issue that you carry – the only one you can predictably, reliably and consistently have any impact upon.

*I Am So Much More:* For about a year, I had the privilege of being in a long-distance relationship with an intriguing and remarkable woman who I'll call Isabella. She reached a point of calling things off. It broke my heart, because I had fallen so deeply in love with her and respected her so much. In the weeks that followed our breakup, she convinced me that we would make much better friends than lovers, so we set out to be great friends. I comforted myself with the knowledge that the love I had experienced with her meant that, beyond a shadow of a doubt, I could love again. I could, in fact, have great love again.

Before we'd called it off as lovers, we had made plans for her to come to Tucson to attend a concert by a musician we both greatly admired. The week before the concert, we agreed by phone that we still wanted to attend the show together. We started the weekend together with a delicious meal out. It was so great to be in her company again. Although I missed the intimate part of our time together, I could see the beauty in the way our relationship had shifted. It allowed for even greater transparency. We didn't have to risk losing the romantic relationship if we told the complete truth. It had already shifted.

Over the course of that first leisurely evening together, we recounted the highs and lows of our short but intense relationship. Being long-distance had meant only being together about once each month. Both of us easily recalled how we would draw closer over the course of a few days. I would feel so close to her that I would want to be as transparent as possible, and I would share truths from my heart that were difficult for her to hear. Her reactions would cause me to pull back, and this sense of not being safe to be totally transparent would stand in the way of our intimacy. She may have experienced my more transparent statements as inexplicable attempts to undermine the energy of the great connection that was underway. With the added perspective of time and our new status as friends rather than sweethearts, I could see that we were in full agreement about our shared and individual parts in the equation.

In remembering my part, I felt a complete lack of defensiveness. I deeply felt the repeated pangs of each moment where I put what, to her, were tacks in the road. I could feel her pain at having our connected energy disrupted and the beauty of our next iterations of trying to make it work. I could feel the recoiling pain I experienced in the wake of each break in the connection. At times, as we laughed and cried over these memories, I could only shake my head in wonder, and with some regret.

I know I am capable of saying things that can be perceived as hurtful. Who hasn't been in that situation – where they think they are merely revealing a level of truth of their own experience? Under those circumstances, I haven't expected those statements to be hurtful; it feels to me like that person can or should be able to handle what I am saying. I find myself surprised when the other person reacts with pain and defensiveness. I also know that as soon as I see I've said something someone else perceives as harmful, I can mindfully choose to reset and be reverent, compassionate and caring. I can do this without wronging myself for having said what was true for me.

I now know I can choose the level of truth and transparency that another person is capable of hearing without triggering defensiveness. This is how I interact with my daughter Alice, so I do know how that feels. Even if it's just a best guess on how to proceed, Alice appreciates my efforts, *and* she appreciates my truth; and I appreciate her truthfulness, too, as well as her great sensitivity to this process.

I didn't succeed in making that choice in my romance with Isabella, but now, I can move the jet fuel of my regrets around that relationship into a stronger commitment to do so in the future. I will find myself tempted to undermine the energetic connection in moments where increasing closeness and intimacy bring out fear and a desire to push the beloved person away. I know I will experience my own humanity, complete with imperfections and rough edges. And I hope to be able to see this, mindfully, well in advance of acting upon it, and to choose wisely to rise to the occasion of greatness, better than ever.

That weekend, despite the joy I experienced with Isabella and the deep, shared understanding we reached, I did have moments where I'd go into a space of being hard on myself. Then, I woke at five in the morning in the midst of a lightning-rod moment. I realized: YES – I had all those ridiculously obvious imperfections of communication that ultimately alienated Isabella, and I may well have my fair share in the future…but I am so much more than that. This was the point in my process of moving on from that relationship where I became increasingly transparent with myself.

I found myself in a beautifully clear space, saying out loud with increasing strength:

I am SO much more.

I AM so much more!

I am so much MORE!

I felt myself claiming my core worth at a level beyond any I'd previously explored.

I am not my imperfection.

I am my greatness.

I am the greatness of worthiness.

I AM SO MUCH MORE.

In the past, I had gone into a space of ruminating over my own perceived imperfections. In that new moment, I chose to reset and claim the greatness of being so much *more* than that.

This saved me the unpleasantness of what I might have chosen to do in the days following: perseverating on my own litany of imperfections and continuing to shake my head at having lost Isabella as a lover. The transformed version, now properly nourished by the primal compost of my frustration, was, "I am the greatness of worthiness. I am the bliss of how that feels. I truly am so much more than the imperfections of the past or any of the future."

Some gardeners say it takes three years for compost to complete its transformation from waste into soil. My great friend Puran Bair created a high-tech scientific process that makes great compost in three days. I say it can be done in our loving hearts in three minutes.

Try it yourself: come up with a few imperfections of your own that have frustrated you in the past. Then, use those very frustrations to lovingly compost more primal nutrition. Build that compost pile and roil it all around. As you  propel your royal nature, know you are *roi-yalty*.

Interesting aside: in the business world, ROI means *return on investment*. Nourish the truth of your worthiness. It will return your investment of energy and focus many-fold.

The transparent truth is:

*You are so much more!*

*You are greatness!*

# Surrendering
# Into Greatness

We tend to think of enlightenment as a state reserved for an exclusive few: people who are blessed with insight or magic that gives them a glimpse into a light the rest of us cannot see. What if enlightenment simply meant being in the light of spirit and in the freedom of playfully exploring greatness – and doing so without being encumbered by feeling less-than in the light?

If we see enlightenment as possible only when our life appears perfect to others or feels perfect to us, we may be sorely disappointed. We may carve out a cave for ourselves that we may never come out of, because why should we bother to reach for the unattainable?

Why not simply envision walking out into the brilliant, inviting and celebrating light that is you? Perhaps that has always been the case – and the task you face is not to find enlightenment, but to get used to the truth: that you are already there.

Greatness is reality. It always has been and always will be. We easily project it on our icons, and it's time to claim for ourselves, too, that greatness that is our birthright.

In sleep, I breathe, and my heart goes on beating and all my organs, tissues and cells, my immune system and all other systems continue to serve their functions. When we sleep, we dream. When we are awake, we see, hear, smell, and taste the world, and these are all miraculous aspects of our greatness. We all have this greatness. If we lost even one of these capacities, we would soon realize just how great are these simple facets of our existence.

The beauty of greatness practice is that we get to design it as we go. Do you want to participate in the designing of your greatness of compassion? In the designing of great qualities such as wisdom, gratitude, power, humor, creativity, imagination? Energize any of these qualities in yourself or in others. To whatever extent you do that – and the sky is the limit – that greatness will become your energetic reality.

It always has been and always will be about choosing. Choosing to reside in the treasure trove of our greatness – not just our own, but that of every person, every living being – rather than sitting outside its door, in the rain, shivering and wishing we could go inside but thinking that the door is locked to us until we find that magical key.

There is no key. The door is open. Stand tall, take a breath, and go inside.

Part Three
# & Beyond...

*The seed of God is in us. Given an intelligent and hard-working farmer, it will thrive and grow up to God, whose seed it is: and accordingly its fruits will be God-nature. Pear seeds into pear trees, nut seeds into nut trees, and God-seed into God.*

- Meister Eckhart, 13th-century mystic

*A seed of God turns into God.*
*Let yourself go, let yourself go...*

- Neil Douglas-Klotz

# Dying to
## the Past

The Nurtured Heart Approach asks us to let go of the past – including the moment just preceding this one. Progressing on this path is, in itself, is a huge undertaking for most people. Most of us learn to ruminate on the *past ad nauseam,* and to reflexively make choices and judgments based on past experience or habit. Letting go of that, to any significant degree, is an important step into trusting one's present circumstances and one's intuition about what is right, right now. It's an important aspect of setting new intentions and acting in accordance with them instead of marching to the beat of a drummer from the distant (or not-so-distant) past. Once that default to the past has been reset to a focus on the present, however, you can return to a whole different kind of examination of the past – one where you set an intention to use the fuel of every bit of the past to create your light of exaltation.

To the extent that you achieve this kind of letting-go – even for a precious few moments – I assure you that you will feel more like the real you than ever. You'll experience yourself in increasingly lit-up ways.

I'll ask you again: how much light did you sign up to carry? Can you trust that, if you use every bit of past as fuel for that fire, you will still be you? We all have our personal histories, and they can be remembered and examined in ways that are useful. The more we can tolerate being unencumbered by the past, the more room we create for revelations from your past to beautifully unfold at just the right time, in harmony with your current level of greatness.

Not long ago, I experienced wave upon wave of strong emotional responses to some events in my life. At times, I felt anguish about how I had let a few things in my life persist and grow as problems. I was angry with myself for ignoring how I'd felt pushed around, and at how I had failed to stand up for what was important to me. Instead, I'd made choices that felt like giving away incremental pieces of myself. As I had these realizations, I saw the repercussions those choices had created over the years. The pattern seemed so obvious. How had I missed it? How had I let things slide so far? They had become blatantly clear in light of the new level of greatness revealed by the practices described in this book.

One day I was really feeling it, resetting the best I could, using the energy to lovingly compost primal nutrition to feed growing greatness. I felt myself bracing for yet another wave of powerful emotion. I was doing the work, and it was beyond any prior level of challenge I had experienced. There had been some great birthing pushes forward, but there I was: yet another day where I was feeling almost overwhelming hurt and anguish. And in that pain, I surrendered and silently asked for help.

I tend not to remember to do this, just as I tend to forget that there's a "help" tab in most software programs. This time, however, when I asked for help, I instantly felt the presence and wisdom of my mother's spirit. She offered these kind words:

"Howard, I am so sorry that I led you to believe that I would only love you if you made choices that ran against who you really are. I see now that those choices caused you to doubt yourself, to lose hold of the real you. I am so sorry. Please forgive me."

This otherworldly acknowledgement and apology caught me completely off guard. In seconds and minutes that followed, so many aspects of my life started to make sense in this subtle new light. In the here and now, I felt the reset of history falling into a new perspective. I felt a true, energetic release of a deep and abiding pattern that had been eroding my day-to-day life; and that, up until that moment, had felt unsettling and undermining. I did need to revisit my past in order to get to that point.

The entire deck of my past reshuffled. A huge weight was lifted. I no longer needed to doubt myself. Having re-cast it as a support for my current greatness, I could energetically release that part of my history and move forward with a new narrative; and I could use the energy of that release to fuel more greatness. And for the first time, I saw that I could truly forgive my mother. I could feel her presence in the room with me as I went through this whole process. "Of course I forgive you, Mom…Of course," I breathed back to her. In the clearing of energies and in my new understanding, I could move forward with the greatness of confidence.

In the course of lots of personal therapy at various times in my life, I had made many attempts to forgive my mother. This was different. This was ten times more real…maybe 100 times more real, and much more powerful. It helped me see that forgiveness is not real until it's *energetically real.*

I came to see the beauty of who she was and how she cared for me, and I could fully thank her; I could more purely see all the other times she had been loving towards me. Prior attempts to forgive her had been out of context: too global, somehow. They had never felt *energetically* complete. This last trip into forgiveness was the one where I found my way into appreciating all she had been. Thank you, Julia Glasser.

An examination of one's personal history can fuel negativity if it unfolds out of context of an intention to use it to fuel greatness in the present. On the other hand, a look at one's personal history can be incredibly productive when it unfolds in harmony with one's ability to handle it and make it useful. A greatness practice can serve the cause of helping old patterning to unfold gracefully and organically in the moment.

# The Michael Jordan
# of ADHD

About 20 years ago, I was invited – along with a half-dozen others – to meet with the marketing director of a local psychiatric facility for children. Others invited included a therapist with a great reputation for her work with blended families; a therapist well-known for her work with step-parenting; another therapist known for work with substance abuse; and yet another therapist whose expertise was in the area of attachment parenting. I was invited due to my emerging reputation for working effectively with children and families dealing with symptoms of ADHD.

Once we were all together, the marketing director explained that they wanted us each to conduct weekly group classes on our respective areas of expertise. We would all be paid the same reasonable fee, and we'd be teaching in rooms they provided on their beautiful campus. They would also market us to the community at large – a nice plus. For them, the win was in offering these classes to the community for free. This generosity reflected well on their commitment to help educate the public and enhanced their positive reputation. Everyone at the meeting agreed to the terms offered. The meeting adjourned on a high note of excitement for what felt like a great win-win opportunity.

About a year later, I ran into the blended-families expert, and we chatted for a few minutes. I knew she was close with several other of the group leaders who had convened that day, so I asked how everyone was doing with their sessions related to this program. I also asked how many people typically attended. To the best of her knowledge, the average attendance per group was ten or less. This immediately got my interest, because the average attendance for my ADHD classes was closer to 100.

I asked the center's marketing director to meet with me, and I pitched the idea that he and his organization were getting much more marketing mileage out of my group compared with the others. I felt that higher compensation was deserved. He disagreed, and gave me the party line of why he couldn't offer me more than he could offer the others. His reply did have merit, but there was something about it that struck a deep chord.

I left his office riled up – more than a little bit righteously indignant. Here's what I ended up saying to myself:

"I know more about ADHD in my little finger than anyone else on the planet. *I am the Michael Jordan of ADHD.*"

In the next moments, I thought, *Whoa! That is a most brash statement.* The truth was that in that moment, I didn't know even a small fraction of what others did about the clinical research on ADHD. I didn't know the party-line medical-model 'facts,' either. What I did know is that I understood and knew these so-called ADHD children at a soul level, and that I was capable of inspiring them to greatness way beyond anyone else I had ever met.

So, I stuck with my audacious Michael Jordan mantra. I let myself own the greatness of my work with ADHD children and the deep understanding that enabled me to do it. More than that: I said it to myself repeatedly and adamantly over the course of the following days and weeks.

I noticed a huge stepping-up into that claim of greatness on my part, leading to several subsequent career leaps. I also noticed a shift in the way the world responded to me and to my knowledge. Getting clear and going to another level of claiming my greatness had taken me to a new and wonderful space of living that greatness within myself and having it seen by my community.

While some might have laughed out loud at or argued against the reality I saw – that I was the Michael Jordan of ADHD – it was simply one way of seeing the truth. There are so many ways of seeing reality. If you go on Google Earth to look at an address, it will look entirely different when you zoom in to see small details than when you zoom back and out to get the broader perspective.

Each increment of that zoom is as real as all the others. All realities are true.

Who possesses out-of-this-world greatness – maybe greatness that has made him or her famous? Use the energy of that person's name, skills and character to amp up your own. Put yourself at that level. Choose to refuse to doubt that you can express just as much greatness. Then, watch the magic happen.

# When Push Comes
# to Shove

Not "living my approach" or "being my approach" is a reference to my not living up to the premises and actions delineated in the Nurtured Heart methodology I developed. I've been accused of this more than once.

I hope that doesn't surprise anyone. I am so human and *so* intense – a true triple Leo. Several people who know the implications of that astrological configuration have told me, "Good luck with that."

It is, in fact, *great* luck, this high-test intensity and humanity, once I get past the surface truth that its challenges can feel like both a blessing and a curse. It carries with it endless opportunities to explore realms of greatness, backed by intense propulsion.

When I catch myself not using the Nurtured Heart Approach – and yes, this does happen – I believe it is because the universe is testing me, yet again, at the highest level so far. It is clear to me that this testing – these challenges – are of my own design and making; and they are always perfectly custom-tailored to push me, once again, out of the womb of what has become comfortable. They propel me out of relative safety and into another level of exploration: further realms of greatness that can take me to even greater levels of manifesting who I have signed on to be.

I must really have something to prove this lifetime. This is the lifetime in which I have little time to waste. It's all about remembering who I really am and acting upon my dreams and visions. This is the lifetime where I get to live my purpose; to really do my job of bringing splendor into form.

I've noticed that as I access ever-sweeter new levels of being and living, the challenges of birthing to next levels do not necessarily get easier. In those moments of recognizing that my boat is about to get seriously rocked, I see myself moving into a period of instability. I know I may be challenged to the core or broken open, and that I might struggle moment-to-moment to reset and stay present in the discomfort of what is old and what is new. Will I rise to the occasion? Depends on whether I am able, once again, to shed life as I have known it.

The Nurtured Heart Approach is relatively simple to apply when things are smooth and life is proceeding in ease and simplicity; the real challenge is to stick to the Stands – actually *notching up* the stands when push comes to shove. (It helps to see the "shove" as the thrust of being born into all that is coming next.)

Each time around the block, the challenges get greater. Each time, my mettle is tested to a greater magnitude. 'Mettle' has a homonym that seems appropriate here: although I haven't worked with metal much, I imagine the final stages of polishing metal to be the most demanding – and that these same efforts lend themselves to the highest levels of glowing illumination.

In those moments where I find my way to the next page of the book of what I've apparently subscribed to, it's as though some power beyond me is asking, "Okay, Sunshine...can you love yourself now? I mean, can you REALLY love *YOU,* under any and all circumstances, even when it feels easy to abandon yourself, to throw yourself under the bus?"

This process isn't nearly as tidy as my prose might suggest. It's about going into a period of relative liminality where I am challenged to the core and sometimes broken open. It usually involves some period of struggling to reset, moment to moment, and to stay present in the discomfort of what is old and what is new. At this edge, I'm often thrown offline to what I aspire to at even my present levels of greatness. Going there begs the question: will this be the level I can't reach? Is this where I can no longer rise to the occasion of what is calling? Is this where I become so weary from the journey that I'd rather just forget the whole thing and go back to old defaults?

Can we rise to this occasion to love parts of us that, at first, might feel unlovable? Can we nurture those parts of ourselves at the most basic, primal level? Can we breathe love into the recesses of our being on blind faith that, in the end, by profoundly loving ourselves, we will be able to go much further in the love we have to give...to everything and anything?

# Luminous
# Lumens

I'd like to invite you to drop into your own unique energetic experience of your body within this greatness practice. Here is where I integrate Greatness Breathing with "luminosity."

I like to imagine that, in addition to the main energy centers such as the chakras described in yoga or the meridians described in traditional Chinese medicine (TCM), many more 'micro-aspects' create energetic systems within our bodies. To me, what is crucially important is the system as a whole. I want to use the vehicle of the breath: inspiring, conspiring and expiring to light up the system as a whole and align with the luminosity of my being. I personally strive to find the register of great being and to match it to luminosity. I occasionally ask myself: how much light do I want to carry? And now, I ask you, how much light do *you* want to carry?

I am convinced that the more conscious light we choose to carry, the more impact we will have in our lives. The scary part of carrying lots of light also means carrying great responsibility. That responsibility often challenges me to my core.

What sparks in me is an image of an old-fashioned light bulb with an arching filament that traverses across its width. There may be many points where energy is more focused between the contacts of electricity, where energy flows from a negatively charged area to a positively charged area (sound familiar?). In the process, bound electrons vibrate at higher levels, subsequently releasing the extra energy in the form of photons that emit light.

The beauty of a light bulb is in the functionality and usefulness of the light. How not-great is a light bulb that doesn't emit light? So, then, how great is it when it consistently and reliably serves its purpose? To me, it's about this very greatness and how we can essentially light up our lives and those of others. Normally I don't worry about the individual chakras, the numerous points on the arch; instead, I use the breath to amplify the overall effect.

I do know that when energy is blocked, stuck places tend to appear at chakra points, and focusing on those points can help things move. This is analogous to the way some teachers of golf like to mechanically break down the swing into many component moves and positions. Addressing particular points along the arc is helpful at times, but no one position will successfully result in the end product of hitting a ball well. It is the moving sum of the parts that creates the fluid movement that delivers that impact.

Not that the study of energy centers from the point of view of any discipline isn't useful. But what I want to achieve is the sum of the parts. And just as there are some phenomenal golfers who probably miss every one of those supposed key junctures of a perfect swing, I think the totality of the luminosity is what has the most powerful impact. I know I need to concentrate on lighting up the full spectrum of lights of my being – the one light that for me is the fluid result of my greatness. My practice here is in a field of luminosity. I go for the big light of greatness, since for me, it projects so much more light inwardly and outwardly, illuminating my way and inspiring the way of my work.

One of the key features of LCD projectors for presentation technology is measured and rated by lumens. Once upon a time, when these machines were in their infancy, the room had to be pretty dark for the colors of slide shows to come through in any degree of vividness. Now, the luminosity of LCDs is high enough to yield vivid color and detail even in brightly lit rooms. That's the degree of luminosity I desire; so I use my imagination to inspire and conspire to qualities of greatness that I can then conspire within and expire out to the world. I use breath to bring this luminosity to the first community of my body and being within, and I use the breath to project these lumens out to the world. I do this both in real time, through my imagination internally, and in real time as life itself is unfolding. If I hit a snag of challenging thoughts and feelings, worry, misery or doubt, I churn these lovingly into fuel for even greater levels of luminosity and greatness.

Here's my luminosity challenge to you: Find your way to a quality of greatness that is meaningful to you at the moment, or let that quality pick you, and then breathe it: inspire, conspire and expire it, while simultaneously infusing it with the light you already carry. Then, light it further with the level of lumens you intuit will project it further into your greater community. After all, you are the presentation and you are the projector. You might as well 'level up' to your greatest luminosity – the one that gets the message of *YOU* out there.

# Growing a
# Backbone

I was at a *Yoga Journal* conference, enjoying a coffee during the morning break. All around me, vendors demonstrated their various yoga-related products. Acrobats on long silks performed inspiring yogic feats in mid-air high above me. Toward the end of the break, the performance ended, and vendors for the food crew began carrying in tables and accessories. I wasn't ready to get up yet, so I stayed in my spot, sitting cross-legged and hunched over, checking e-mails. Then, right near me, there was a huge crash.

A glass and metal cooler case loaded with sodas had fallen just a foot or two away from me, glass side first. As I looked up, my life flashed before my eyes. I had just been spared grave injury, or worse. The sense of what could have happened – but didn't – kept energetically perseverating throughout the minutes that followed.

Luckily, some new friends saw what happened and came to check in with me. As we walked over to where the next classes took place, I got to process a bit of what I was feeling, although still in that bewildering space of shock and bliss at the near-miss that, to me, seemed like it must have involved some kind of angelic intervention. In this softened, altered state, I stepped into an incredible yoga class with husband-and-wife teachers, whose focus was a practice called Deep Yoga. The practice was devoted to honoring one's self while in the flow of poses.

The teachers asked us to consider what quality would perfectly serve our lives right now. What came to mind immediately was a version of the deep gratitude I had been feeling since that close call just minutes before: *great-full-ness*. As I held this word in my mind and heart, I felt lit up from my core.

During an inspiring moment a few minutes later, I could feel a twitch in the backache that had been my nagging companion for the last few weeks. Then, in a moment of clarity, as I invoked and claimed a bit more of my newfound 'fullness' of great qualities that I possess, I felt a sensation in my back that I can best describe as *clear*. It felt like a portion of my spine was elongating enough to gain a few degrees of relief.

I thought of the link between great-full-ness and my back. I could sense how my back had, over the years, become compressed with non-great-full-ness. I also now vividly knew that filling my spinal cord – the vital center of the back that has carried me though so much, the back that could have been crushed just minutes earlier – with grate-full-ness would revitalize my spine to full length and full blessed health.

How would I remember great-full-ness this time? Would I need yet another close call to remember? Or could I find the audacity to stay with what I had now stumbled upon?

I knew I might forget. A few years before, I had a similar instance of being in a situation where I miraculously escaped harm. At the time, I felt profoundly grateful, but since then the strength of that feeling had dissipated. It flashed into my mind that if I could see this quality as *great-full* instead of grateful, that the extra "L" could serve as a kind of anchor to that sensation of great-full-ness itself elongating my back. I played around with *realllllllllly* expanding those *L's*. I saw how this could be worked into an expansive sense in other realms of my practice.

As yoga class ended, I lay flat on my back and purposefully extended inner self-recognition in a manner reminiscent of that long, rolling series of L's. Instead of saying internally that I am loving, or the greatness of loving, I said to myself: *I am the greatness of being audaciously and unapologetically loving.* In my mind, I fleshed this out even further by adding appreciative detail to my intention and ways of being loving. I elongated and gave texture to the explanation, boosting the appreciation and gratitude already there to another level entirely. It was delightful

– blissful, like an internal massage of my spinal cord! The painful compression I had felt was further released. I had a distinct inner experience of my spine becoming longer. I was amazed, and still am, at the power of inner recognition to positively affect my physical well-being. My core truly felt *full* of greatness.

When I first brought the Nurtured Heart Approach into the world in the mid-1990s, I would speak to children appreciatively, giving detailed recognitions and acknowledgements. Then, after my lightning strikes a few years later and my eventual personal exploration of greatness, I began to feel compelled to tell children about the greatness I witnessed in them. Having seen so many children rise, expand and blossom in response to my words, I came to feel as though I had found a way to talk directly to their souls. It was clear that these words of greatness registered profoundly in their spirits. Before my eyes, they sat up taller – they appeared to actually grow in response to my reflections. That day, using this resonant mode of reflection on myself, I felt the very same experience deep inside my own being.

For now, I choose to refer to this experience as 'growing a backbone.' This fairly common expression has been used to describe an increase of inner strength, with an underlying implication of "you are clearly, right now, *not strong enough.*" In this context, I see the finding of one's greatness as a way of building real inner strength upon the strength that is already there. No lack is implied – it's an expansion, a fortification that does not require a sacrifice of fluidity or movement.

Let your instincts assist you in creating a simple method for remembering to fill yourself with greatness. This is not about obtaining something that's absent, but about remembering who you really are.

# Judging In
## Greatness

When we choose to complain, we 'pay' with our energy for the privilege of the flow of complaints. In complaint, we remain at cross-purposes, communicating an upside-down energetic message: that we love complaining, and that we love whatever we are complaining about. We step into the shared trance where problems bring us the juiciest version of connected relationship.

When you feel like complaining about someone else's bad attitude, what ideal do you wish she was living up to? Maybe you have a belief that she ought to be respectful of others. Rather than energizing the *lack* of that value, find ways in which she is already being respectful. To what degree is she respectful to others? Even the smallest trace of respect or lack of disrespect yields abundant opportunity to appreciate her respectfulness. Energize the ideal of what you wanted in the first place. Give that your energy, then watch it grow.

Use any complaint as an internal cue to find some trace of what you're seeking; and to put your attention there, on what you *do* want. Just remember these two steps:

1. Reset.

2. Renew. Take the energy of that complaint and transform it. Give some thought to what ideal you are seeing buried within the complaint you were preparing to voice. Find examples of that ideal in your current Now – and in the Nows that follow.

# The Web of
## Commitment

Recently I noticed that I had fallen into a pattern of waking in the night, then allowing the beginnings of negative thoughts to migrate into the inner conversations I was conducting with myself. I would find myself needing to reset – often repeatedly, in a short span of time – and then I would use that energy to shoot for more exploration of greatness. Yes, I was living my method, but I was doing so at the expense of my sleep being disturbed.

What I clearly came to notice: 1) there was always a moment or more of warning, where I would sense the impending wave of negative thought; and 2) in my choice to entertain the thought even a little bit, even if I was resetting to the fullest and making gains as a result of the greatness "jet fuel" I called up following the reset, I still was paying a price. I was wearing myself out physically and emotionally with these extended periods of sleeplessness, and I was breaking an even bigger commitment that I wasn't yet quite aware of.

I made a commitment to myself that if I woke in the middle of the night, I would not give a moment's airtime or an ounce of energy to negative thoughts. Instead, I committed to getting out of bed and sitting quietly in meditation when I felt even an inkling of the first sign of negativity rolling in. Immediately, it was evident that in sitting up in this committed way, I was better at not giving any energy to whatever wave of bother wandered into my mind. What was even more evident is that by not giving any airtime to problems, I was able to visit a very different space in these contemplative periods. Each time, I found that something important would always come through to me – messages from the universe that downloaded into my consciousness, gifts of valuable, positive inner advice.

Many of the pieces that became this book arrived in this way: I woke late at night, got right out of bed, sat in meditation, refused to entertain even the tiniest negative thoughts, and listened for downloads. For five nights in a row after starting this new practice, I generated this and three other chapters of this book. It was a simple, amazing flow. The words just came. Then, I fell into a deep, unburdened sleep.

And then, one night, in the most obvious and almost overtly defiant way, just before bedtime, I blatantly broke a different commitment to myself. I don't recall which commitment I broke; it might have been my commitment to not eat before bedtime or to avoid refined sugar. Whatever the details, the vibrational vector of my word to myself – the energy of which translates to life force, light and love transmitted – was devalued.

Fast-forward to four hours later, when I woke up in the dead of night. There I was, face to face with my commitment to get out of bed every time this happened. The previous few nights, it had been relatively easy to get up to sit in contemplation; my commitment had felt strong and clear. This night, though, I really did *not* want to get up. I even briefly entertained letting the negative thought have the old little bit of airtime. At that point, the universe supplied some interesting background sounds that helped me ignite greatness through the commitment I had made.

I live in the desert of Tucson, Arizona; not in the city proper, but out on the range. That night's background music came from my neighbors, the coyotes, who were right in the process of making a kill. When they surround the desert animal they scare up, they howl in an eerie, ritualistic fashion just before they pounce on their dinner. I'm sure I sleep through several such happenings in the course of a normal night, but this one was close, and particularly loud.

This extra background noise supported me in upholding my commitment to getting out of bed and (I hoped) receiving the gift of words like those you are reading now. The timing was perfect. If it hadn't been for those coyotes howling so close by, I might well have stayed in bed and reverted to my former way of resetting the negativity that was clearly on its way.

Later on, I realized that if I had chosen to stay in bed that night, it would have had to do with the commitment I had broken before going to sleep. I had defused the energy of commitment in a general way, and this could easily have impacted other commitments I had made. Because we live in a world where most of us – at least sometimes – make commitments we do not or cannot keep, this seemed important. Commitments are essentially the stands we take.

What was revealed to me this was that honoring our word to ourselves is an important way we maintain our vital force. With every commitment we keep with ourselves, our impact and energy in terms of future commitments is enhanced. If we undermine our impact in one realm – even if it seems, at first, to be relatively private or insignificant – it is connected by invisible threads to other realms of our lives and to the energies that support our other endeavors.

When we speak to another person or tackle a job, we really do want it go well, whether we think about that each time or not, and whether we are doing something mundane (washing the dishes) or important (having a challenging conversation with someone we love). If our essential energies are dissipated by one aspect of our existence, and if that negatively affects other aspects, then isn't that reason enough to consider the greater importance of our commitments?

Commitment is about being able to trust your word to yourself and others. This trust allows you to relax in respect to the things to which you 'give your word.' Failure to keep commitments small or large might well keep us in the revolving door of life: the cosmic treadmill of Groundhogs' Day.

Considering these words, shifting my perspective, and seeing in this an entirely new way everything is connected by energy, I am re-committing now to keeping all my commitments. At some later date I'll let you know how it goes. That's a commitment. And I am a man of the ever-increasing energy of my word.

# Waiting for
# Rodriguez

*Searching for Sugar Man* is a 2012 Swedish–British documentary directed and written by Malik Bendjelloul. It details the efforts of two South African musicologists to find out whether the rumored death of Detroit singer-songwriter Sixto Rodriguez had actually happened; and, if not, to discover what had become of him.

Rodriguez's music never took off in the United States, but became wildly popular in South Africa – supposedly outselling the Beatles and Rolling Stones combined. As his songs became anthems for the South African anti-apartheid movement, he vanished from public view; the only clues about what might have become of him came in bits and pieces from the liner notes of his album.

Just as these Cape Town musicologists gave up on finding Rodriguez, one of their online attempts at outreach miraculously found its way to his daughter. She called them, beginning a series of unlikely events that eventually led to Rodriguez being brought to South Africa with his daughters to play his music. This humble man believed that he'd be performing for small groups of people in honkytonks or other small venues, as he had done in the past.

Rodriguez had given up on performing. For years, he had been supporting his daughters by laboring as a demolition worker in inner city Detroit. Even as he carried refrigerators down tenement stairs on his back, he always dressed in the most dignified ways and conducted himself in greatness. Although he had faced the reality of his music not selling in the States and had done what he needed to do to earn a living, he had never given up on greatness.

As the movie ends, Rodriguez emerges into the truth of the greatness he has been able to express through his music. At his concerts, he and his family are blown away when huge crowds of adoring fans show up to see him play. In one filmed segment, when he finally comes out on stage, the fans can't bring themselves to end their applause despite multiple attempts to begin the song. This man, who had never performed for large crowds prior to this, just waited in the most poised way; eventually, he was able to begin the concert. He conducted himself as though he had done this a million times – as if greatness had always been his fate. I believe it was: that it was waiting for him across a few bodies of water, in a country where one bootlegged album began a groundswell of inspiration completely by word of mouth.

This multiple award-winning documentary has struck a chord for so many people. It's an incredible illustration of the way in which being true to one's self, and in which living in greatness no matter what our circumstances, leads us to more greatness. This is a story about the greatness waiting for every one of us. As we listen and remember who we really are and live in simple accordance with what is true for us, we find our own greatness, and it finds us.

# Married to
# Yourself

We all know the dismal statistics on marriage in the U.S.: 50 percent of marriages end in divorce; some 70 percent of second or third marriages fail. It may be that we're expecting too much from that institution. Maybe "'til death do us part" isn't feasible in the world we live in now, with our very long lifespans and the complexities of modern life. Perhaps we've heaped unreasonable expectations upon marriage as a linchpin of family and society. That being said, and with open admission that I may not be the best authority on marriage (I was married and divorced and have not been married since, nor do I especially want to be), I have some ideas about why we find ourselves in this place where divorce is so common.

Most of us haven't learned to be "married" to *ourselves* first – before we say "I do" to someone else. Many of us have a habit of putting our own needs last; of being cruel to ourselves through our self-talk; of pushing ourselves harder than we'd ever push anyone else; or of sacrificing our own well-being or safety. Most of us don't learn to love, honor and obey ourselves before we vow to do so with another. Talk-show talking heads and women's magazines constantly advise us to take "me time" and "put ourselves first." Without a dedicated practice, however, it's hard to do anything but pay this notion lip service. Greatness practice is an actual way to honor your commitments to yourself, every day – especially when faced with challenges.

Maybe our first marriage should be to ourselves. We could vow to truly be there for ourselves and to refuse to throw ourselves under the bus at any time, especially when things get tough. To vow to be accepting and kind, to obey our intuitive hits on what is best for us, to refuse to beat up on ourselves over our mistakes, and to take excellent care of our bodies whether they are sick or well? What if we promised ourselves to stick with ourselves through thick and thin; to honor and cherish greatness through wealth and poverty, sickness and health, to death do us part - on an internal level?

# Apologies
# Unaccepted

Do you ever toss out "I'm sorry"s like confetti? Does this readiness to apologize make you feel like you are coming across as a nice person, a giving person – perhaps as a person who is exquisitely sensitive to and regretful for any damage he or she has done to another?

Maybe even the temptation to say "I'm sorry" is best understood as a desire to bring oneself to the *next level of greatness*. It's a reflection of an inner recognition that it exists and awaits, and that you are edging toward the point from which you can jump.

My 'best' at any given moment is tied tightly to my current level of greatness and inner wealth. That's all I can bring to the table. If life shows me patches where that level doesn't quite match my endeavors, then all I need to do is go back to work invoking the next levels of greatness. If something is not manifesting the way I want it to at the current level of greatness, I turn up the dial.

My overwhelming experience with 'greatness downloads' is that they come bundled with sensitivity to others, to society and to the world at large. The needs of the planet, the environment and the situation are all addressed organically. If my heart remains open, it will notify me when my current operating level of greatness is falling short. When this happens, all I have to do is 'go online' to find the next upgrade.

You can do this responsively, when the situation or your heart demands an amped-up level of greatness; or you can do it proactively, out of curiosity about the next horizon of greatness.

This being said, it may turn out to be appropriate to apologize from time to time to admit discourtesy or error. If you do so, do it consciously, and stop at "I'm sorry" or "I messed up here. I take responsibility." Forego any explanation or excuses. Treat the urge to say "I'm sorry" as a reset to greatness, just as you might treat the urge to say "thank you" as a reminder to reset to a further explanation of your gratitude. Renew to remembering who you really are. Jump further into greatness.

# Unfolding in
# Perfection

When people come to our intensive week of training in the Nurtured Heart Approach, there comes a point in the week where some of those in the room realize that they will be facing big issues in their lives when they get home. They see that if they are going to fulfill a commitment to parenting or teaching using this approach, they will encounter no small amount of pushback from family, friends, and colleagues. They want to proceed, but they are sometimes scared, and they tend to have a lot of questions about how to navigate the conversations and confrontations they are imagining. They want our help to prepare themselves.

We do prepare them, but not by figuring out good retorts to the inevitable critiques and questions people will have about this approach. The most important job of the person bringing this back home is to grow his or her own greatness. In focusing on this, the person will communicate all that needs communicating.

I encourage and teach people to reset from doubts about how they will manage this transition…right back into true appreciation of the great qualities that they already are. As they encounter negative feelings or stories from themselves or others, they are then inspired to reset and continue to accrue more inner wealth.

People often come away from these trainings feeling downright fervent, ready to give negativity the boot wherever they might see it and to walk away from people who won't get on board with what they've discovered. I tell them that they don't have to go home and say goodbye on day one to the people, places and things that no longer serve them. These realms will reveal themselves over time, as will the perfect timing of steps to be taken, should they prove necessary. Lines that need to be drawn simply appear.

Half the time, people you don't expect to get on board with this level of positivity actually sense your new clarity and respond in the positive ways you would have wanted in the first place. In my own experience, I have often found that out of my increasing inner wealth and greatness, I come to see people, places or things in a greater light as well, and any need I have to see them behave differently fades from the picture.

I have also found that as I progress in levels of clarity – as I refuse ever more staunchly to go into negativity, choosing instead to go further into greatness – that the people, places and things that need to fall away tend to fall away on their own. Scenarios tend to emerge that make this inevitable.

I always default to breathing into my greatness. That is the true reset: remembering who you really are, as a person of greatness. If I stick with that default, even the tough work of drawing boundaries, walking away from relationships that aren't working, or managing a difficult transition becomes graceful and clean. Changes happen in perfect orchestration with the level of inner greatness I need to handle the whole situation. Even if this kind of equanimity seemed out of reach just a short while ago, here it is now, unfolding in perfection. Even if it hurts like crazy, here I am, handling it, using the inner strength I have cultivated over these last hours, days, weeks, and years.

As you recognize yourself in this space, know that even if in the past you never thought such a change possible, here you are, living your way into it. It's not a question of whether you can or can't; you *are*. You are the greatness of wisdom. You know what is perfect for you. You are remembering the constellation of greatness that is you and that has always been. You are remembering who you are as a person of greatness; not merely who you might have previously been led to believe was you, not who you thought you were, but truer and truer each day to who you really are in that growing light of living out your dreams, living in your passions and expressing your true self.

# Being
# Ripped

So often, when the going is rough, we'd rather be anywhere but here, in this moment of intense vulnerability, curiosity, wonder, and fear. When obstacles roll in, we may experience variations and degrees of heartbreak – always a potent catalyst of growth, but seldom a welcome guest. Do we have the courage to truly be in that moment where we're ripped open, and to view it as an opportunity for growth into next levels of greatness? Some days, yes; other days, not so much. Either way, heartbreak will always come again, and with it, opportunity to 'get ripped' in a way that doesn't involve steroids or heavy weights.

In common parlance, being 'ripped' denotes having bulging muscles with great definition. I'm exploring a new way of using this term: to describe this state of being broken open, afraid, inspired, and intoxicated to the core. I haven't yet heard a word that satisfactorily describes this state, so I'm proposing that if I'm in it, I'm *ripped*. The narrative I am creating is that this is an alternative way of being muscular and powerful.

I know firsthand that having one's heart broken can feel devastating: like splitting wide open – a state of vivid, wild vulnerability. In the aftermath, however, many experience a renewed lease on life and rise to better-than-ever ways of living. Others never really recover. I'm sure the same is true for loss of love and loss of loved ones. But according to my new definition of being ripped, the prospects of propelled growth leading to next levels of greatness are vast. Making those levels accessible requires only a perspective that even heartbreak is a kind of reset that will lead us there.

# Following Your
## Inner Wisdom

In 2011, my daughter was enrolled in an honors program abroad as part of her junior year at Rhode Island School of Design. I visited her in Rome. Together, we took in the sights and sounds of many buzzing neighborhoods; we enjoyed cappuccino, gelato, and even a few glasses of wine (she had just turned 21) at her favorite places. One day, she had a pressing assignment to work on. She suggested that I take a walk to the Colosseum while she worked. It was, she said, a pretty straightforward stroll of a mile or so away.

Off I strolled, and when I got there, I gazed in amazement. It was so impressive. I walked around the outside, drinking in the scope, scale and magnitude of the architecture, imagining all the work that had gone into its preservation. I came back around to the front and decided to get in line for inside access. Just thirty seconds into being in the line in the afternoon heat, I did a startled double-take when stern words of direction came from deep inside my being. Strong and clear, I heard:

*"Don't you dare go in there."*

It was far from the first time I'd heard such words of guidance, but these were adamant. I knew better than to go against them. Within a minute of following this direction, I was given a gift of knowledge: *the Colosseum was one of the places where violence for entertainment was born.*

This wave of knowledge/knowing threw me off just a bit. I don't believe I had ever thought about this before that time, although I'd known about the Colosseum and its historical significance for most of my adult life.

Soon after that came another wave: a visualization of what those times must have been like. I was given a viscerally affecting glimpse into that time in Roman history: the terror and horror of those used for entertainment, and the cheering throngs who created demand for this form of entertainment merely by being there. I can't say whether it was historically accurate, but it gave me what I sensed as the essence of the anguish of that period.

Alongside this, I saw parallels in some of the ways modern society perpetuates that tradition. A 'video' began to play in my mind. It went through a series of formats reminiscent of sports, cinema, advertisement-driven television and pay-per-view scenarios. The theme that ran through it all: the ways we show up to watch hurt, degradation, loss and anguish. This is so much a habit in our culture that the fact that we do this and the impact it has usually hits well below our radar. This precise, directive inner multimedia show gave me beautifully timed guidance. It deepened my understanding of how important my work is in changing these defaults that date at least back to the Roman Empire.

I have come to value these kinds of "downloads" as great gifts, and I have learned (the hard way) to heed, appreciate and abide by their wisdom. In welcoming such guidance, I open up to a channel of reception that has always been there. All I have to do is tune in and follow it to its logical, wise conclusions. Being open to experiencing and following my intuitive "hits" has immeasurably increased my attunement to the long-sought truth of who I am and how I wish to be in the world. It has allowed those "hits" to go from small physical impulses or inklings to full-scale multimedia visualizations, with a concomitant increase in the density of the detailed information they yield. It gives me a glimpse into how much farther I go beyond my previous small ideas of myself.

Following this kind of guidance can feel scary. Not going into the Colosseum that day wasn't a big deal, because I was alone; but what if I'd been with a big group of family members and friends eager to explore the inside of this historic monument? What would they have thought of me if I'd turned on my heel and taken off, saying that I just couldn't go inside? Would they feel judged by me if they were to go in? A tough conversation might have been called for in that moment. Shifting the context, I can recall so many other instances where I had to rock the boat because my intuition guided me away from some expected action, relationship or choice. Unless you're a true solo act, rocking the boat always rocks others' worlds, and sometimes that meets with pushback, criticism or hurt feelings.

When I feel that fear, I remind myself that my highest intention is exploring and awakening greatness, and that all good and great things I wish for will come from that higher intention as I hold it clearly and enact it cleanly. If, in this exploration, I can use life's challenges and life's circumstances to gain access to any next level of truth and any next level of greatness, I can be that much more clear and loving to myself and others. Compassionately understanding and acting from deeper levels of personal truth helps me actualize as a great person making great contributions via an increasingly purposeful life. Even if there is disruption at some level as a result, in the end, it works itself out for the best.

Listen to your inner voice that much more carefully. It's always there, open for questions…and answers. The further you dive into greatness, building inner wealth, the more you will trust it; and the more comfort you will find in resetting to the knowing that follows.

# Here Comes
# the Sun

One bright, brisk early morning, I was standing on the patio outside my room, doing a few yoga-style stretches and having a few mindful moments in the splendor of the Arizona sun. I realized that even as a young child, I must have been trying to access this splendor. Like so many people I know who grew up before we knew the dangers of sun damage, we would bake ourselves in the hot summer sun for long periods of time. In that moment, decades later, I saw that the allure may have been this beautiful connection to the blazing light of the sun. I let myself feel that connection fully.

It was a sublime moment, a holy moment where I felt tuned in to something vast, but that I also sensed existed entirely within me. It was a moment of blissful oneness, where my own greatness was indistinguishable from the greatness from which I came and into which I'll eventually dissolve.

I often experience these kinds of moments of truth in the quiet of meditation or the peace of the early morning. Up bubbles a deeper experience of the greatness of love, compassion, connection, or wisdom. In the aftermath, as I figuratively shake myself off and get ready to go back into my day and all its responsibilities and logistics, how do I make that so real on the inside that it manifests there, too, in my everyday life? In other words: on Monday morning, when the gravity of my life takes hold, how am I going to put what I learned in the peaceful moments of retreat into play?

It can be hard to find your way to what is sacred and holy in the real world. It's easy to come across *reminders* of what's holy – inspiring messages, imploring sermons, admonitions and inspiring readings, and other hints and references to experiences that are deeply sacred – but the actual experience of the holy tends to be elusive in our day-to-day lives. I want smooth, easy access to deeply spiritual moments like the one I experienced on my patio that sunny morning. I want that in every context. I explore greatness work as a way to achieve this.

The greatness practice also leads to loving interchanges with others, for example, that yield magical moments of intimacy as both people acknowledge and appreciate greatness. Being in and appreciating the greatness of mindful silence, mindful sounds and rhythms, mindful movement and activity, mindful work, mindful exploring of art, music, exercise, faith, nourishment, nature, and spirit all serve to enhance our everyday experience of the holy.

Celebrating your own greatness through focused, creative, expansive recognitions is a way to 'be' the experience of holiness – to revisit it at will. Your experience will not be like mine; it will be your own personal experience of the sacred, based on your own way of celebrating it via word, breath and intention. Appreciation and gratitude are choices I make that help keep that doorway to the sacred, to the holy, open – even in the course of my everyday life.

# Singing Your Name:
# The Advanced Variation

et's say that lately, I am intentionally invoking the greatness of truth. Let's say I have seen this as an important quality in my life, and it has challenged me in numerous contexts. Let's say it has inspired me to intentionally *breathe* into deeper and deeper levels of truth.

Through my breath, I nourish this quality in my heart. Through appreciation of the greatness of truth I already have, and through gratitude for my courage in looking further to deeper levels of personal truth, I am conspiring, in my heart, to ever-greater levels of truth. With this comes a sacred inner sense of owning the quality in my heart: I find expansive new experiences of *being the greatness of truth.*

Then, I follow the route of this soulful breathing by expiring: moving this mindful heart energy out into the world. With it, I infuse every last fiber of my existence: every cell, muscle, and space in the universe of my being. And let's say that through this process, I receive a sacred call back, with a series of questions that challenge this process:

"To what extent of 'great' are you owning this quality of truth?"

Let's say I reflexively respond: "Very great."

Then comes, "Define *very great.*"

I respond, "Majestically great," thinking at the level of royalty.

Then comes, "…and what level is that?"

"Howard Neil Glasser great!" I respond. This feels just right.

What if our names were the perfect definition of our own personal constellations of greatness? What if our names could serve as unique mantras to help us recall the greatness we've signed up for in this lifetime?

Your name holds a unique vibrational register. You can use

your name to remember who you are and to step up to the plate of your commitment to *being* that greatness. We use our own names, hear our names spoken, and read our own names many times each day. If you choose to designate your name as a reminder to perpetuate any quality of greatness that you wish to express, imagine how many times each day you'll be gently guided back into your own greatness!

You can even sing your name to the tune of any song that inspires you. I've been singing that song to different melodies for a few years now, and this has helped me stay conscious of that song as a representation of my dogged determination to bring splendor into form. I've even found myself singing these songs when I wake in the middle of the night.

As soon as I experience the nectar of spirit in these forms of greatness, I want to test whether I can remember to stay in the sacred once I'm out in the world. I want to see how this impacts my interactions with all the people, places and things already in my life – what fun! I get to see how "cooked" the quality in question is for me, and how much more work might be needed. I see old forms and formats of my existence falling away and the formation of new and welcome pieces of the puzzle.

Is this completely crazy – or a tribute to my work and to my purposeful commitment? Since I get to choose which story I believe, I'll stick with the latter narrative.

For the fun of it: choose to sing your name to any tune you desire. Choose to associate it with your growing constellation of greatness. When anything less than greatness wags its tail at you, choose to use your growing array of reset practices. Choose to experience references to your name as a reminder of who you really are.

# On Taking Our
# Breath Away

The night before I wrote this chapter, I was out to dinner with three friends while visiting my cousin Alec. As we shared stories and laughter, Alec's neighbor came up to our table to say hello. This lovely woman introduced us all to her husband and her other friends, a group that included another woman who looked like an amalgam of so many great people I had met in my life. I knew I didn't know her but I felt I had known her forever.

That experience was – for lack of a more conventionally accepted word – *spacious*. It took my breath away, and as I felt it, I knew everyone else at the table felt it, too. I took the risk of honestly putting words to the truth of my experience. Transparently, I told her, "You took my breath away." Later on, my cousin could not stop talking about how moved he was by my daring to utter those simple words in the truth of that beautiful moment.

The next morning, I wondered and pondered in the wake of that thrilling experience. *Can we find our own being to be breathtaking? I asked myself. Can we love ourselves that profoundly? Can we love all of humanity in that same way?*

In our culture, some lip service is paid to self-love, but the bottom line is that we are often shamed for openly, bountifully loving ourselves. Think of a public figure, friend, or family member who really walks the talk of self-love, and think about how they tend to be regarded by you or others. They're seen as a little weird, a little "off." Our culture is far from encouraging a living kind of self-love that matches or exceeds our expressions of love for others.

This kind of love is expressed by treating all circumstances that come our way with an ever-loving heart. Can we experience all that flows into and out of our lives…in love? Can we feel it all

– every last bit – without abandoning ourselves? Better yet, can we breathe it all *in, in love,* never exiting a state of appreciation and gratitude for each and every feeling and experience – even the challenging ones? And then, in that space of love, acting with intention to extract the gold, greatness, and *'godness'* from it all? That's the alchemy. That's the magic.

If you've noticed, Buddha consciousness, Krishna consciousness, Christ consciousness and other transcendental vantage points are similar in that they are profoundly loving and profoundly compelling. The theologies and cultural foundations of these traditions profoundly differ from one another, but in all their descriptions of the experience of love, they are all simply urging us to find that same vantage point for ourselves.

I'll venture that all of these important spiritual teachers/deities wanted most for us to profoundly, deeply and fully love ourselves, each other, and all of humanity. A tall order – not for the faint of heart, but utterly doable. Like every great journey of attainment, it begins with a single step, starting in exactly the place where we find ourselves when we realize we must begin.

I took that first step at the start of this century, when I began to play with turning the approach I developed for others onto myself. I found myself fiercely devoted to seeing where this path has led. It's always and only led to more exploring. It's always led to more doorways worth moving through. It has always led me ultimately into finding out who I really am and away from who I thought I was. It has always led to this moment in time of this most enjoyable part of the journey when so much else that obstructed the view was pared away. My exploration now is truly joyful in exploring the glory of profound love of self, others and humanity. It captivates me and takes my breath away every bit as much as falling in love in the more traditional sense.

# Me Through
# **You**

"**M**e through you." These three words kept coming to me, over and over. I had no idea what this 'transmission' meant or what I was supposed to make of it. One day, it occurred to me to ask what this was about, and to my delight and surprise, I got an answer. This led me into an extended Q&A with whatever powers create these downloads in my mind. It was all I could do to keep up with it, but I did manage to write most of it down.

**What do you mean by 'me through you'?**

*If I were the voice of the universe, I would communicate me through you. I would give you ways and words that would support you in making your life an inspiring expression of my nature. Your explorations would show me all of life's possibilities. Your greatness would be celebrated and, in turn, would inspire more greatness.*

*Greatness is the root system we all have in common. Like the water lilies on the pond, we are all linked at our roots. We all share the common destiny of blossoming into our greatness. As you do, so do I. As I do, so do you. I love what is possible. This, alone, is my fascination and my quest.*

*Some of you need adversity to reveal further greatness. That's why I give you plenty of adversity – why wouldn't I give you that opportunity? Really, it's my opportunity too – to further cherish and guide you. I'm so eager to see you blossom that I might send a lot of adversity your way to make it happen. Wars, destruction, pandemics...I don't stop at anything to give you the opportunity to see me in you, gloriously. It's all in service to you all finding the greatness that is already alive in you.*

*Would I prefer you take it upon yourselves to find this glory? Absolutely. I would cherish each and every unprovoked step you take in the direction of greatness. I would give you lots of signs so you'd know how pleased I was. I would lean all the way into that conversation, because it's what I would consider a real conversation: a furthering of who you really are that comes forth as you build clarity and confidence, and then a carrying of this out to others. This is the revolution of greatness that I aspire to – that I am inspiring to. This is the revolution I want to take to the streets; the one I dream of continually. This is behind everything I do. It is my one and only intention and the purpose of all my actions.*

**So: I am the greatness of listening intently, and the greatness of choosing to believe what is there?**

*This makes me happy, that you see the beauty and greatness in this. I feel like an inventor who has only been able to envision the basic circuitry of a project – enough to bring it to life – and who has had the privilege of witnessing as it springs to much more surprising, intense, amazing life, something beyond my wildest dreams.*

**What do you mean by "my wildest dreams?"**

*I feel so happy when I see flowers blooming. So many of these flowers are astonishingly beautiful – beyond my wildest dreams. In the same way, when any of the people of the world blossom, I feel that same delighted surprise. I celebrate all I see in this direction. It makes me so happy. I rejoice when people awaken to who they really are, even if it happens in the smallest of ways. Their greatness is their divinity.*

**Even in the smallest ways?**

*I celebrate even the tiniest movements beings take in the direction of embracing their divinity. I open my heart in love. My being blossoms. This is how I have fun! I experience myself, my 'god-ness,' through you and others.*

**You experience yourself through others…What can I do that will make you rejoice?**

*I love it when your fear dissolves, or when you check your fear at the door and allow yourself to openly explore your being in this world. It becomes a world full of gifts and love, and I rejoice for you as well as for myself, because I feel those gifts so deeply.*

*I even feel your sexuality. I experience your longing, your desire, your ecstasy in your body, heart and soul, because I live in your body. I am your body. I am your heart. I am your soul. I experience your ecstasy. I am that, for every living creature.*

*So many of you let fears, worries and doubts get in the way of fully feeling your desire. I need you to feel it all for me – to not let fear get in the way. Can you imagine the joy I feel when someone is willing to explore it all? Can you imagine how that is multiplied when someone moves into a place of alignment with who he or she really is as a person of greatness? Imagine how it feels to me as I watch them explore. That's where I truly see what is possible. I cannot do that without you. You all are my means of exploration.*

*When you try on any of the stellar qualities programmed into your design, I rejoice. When you activate or 'program' for yourself any quality new to me – one I have not yet seen or conceived of – I feel it deeply, and I rejoice. As you actualize your own unique version of even a common quality, it is very new to me, and I experience it deeply, and I rejoice. And when you purposely play with the edges of that quality as you bring it to life, and as you bring it to your life, I feel it deeply…and I rejoice.*

*Can you imagine this? If you can, you are experiencing, right this moment, me through you. You are experiencing the design of my creation. You are experiencing my joy.*

**Joy?**

*My joy is so easy to come by. I am happy when someone does something good, but I am overjoyed when someone decides to live great, think great, see great…live great. As they choose to explore and manifest all they can be at this point in time, I see my plan unfold beyond anything I could have imagined.*

*The real breakthroughs come when a person goes to a personal best in any quality of greatness. It's always going to ripple out and inspire others to live greatness, and this is what inspires me. And joy is my normal state of knowing that this is happening, or is about to happen. The joy of knowing that the limits of greatness are about to expand is deliciously exciting for me. I love when beings conspire to create more or further greatness, individually or in groups. I can't ever force anyone to take this route, but I can optimize circumstances.*

*Even areas of life that people might think to be outside this realm of exploration and joy are, in fact, well within this arena. Sexuality, relationships, business, sports...nothing is excluded. All are areas where you can explore the depth, width, breadth and intensity of emotion, determination, tenacity and love. It is all endlessly fascinating to me.*

*How can you explore your edges of greatness in any of this? Only in your own very unique way. This multiplies my excitement about seven billion-fold! The explicit beauty in all of this is that it can't help but occur through the particular filter of YOU and how you see the world.*

*If you are holding on to suppositions about how the world is supposed to be; if you are living by the edicts of organized philosophies or traditions – then the dust of that can settle on your filters and restrict your explorations of greatness. If everyone lived out the same notion of what makes a good life or what expresses greatness, my view of the possibilities of goodness and greatness would be constricted. If everyone honored their own heart and their own dreams and made this the central philosophy, tradition, and passionate driving force of their lives, there would be so much more exploration of greatness within each individual. I would have so much more to be excited about.*

*If a dictator were to issue a mandate requiring everyone in his country to live in a tightly regulated manner – if they were told how to have friendships, how to work, how to create and how to love – the only new explorations would come from those who rebelled. I've seen this happen in various parts of the world, and it has helped me to measure what I truly value: and that is freedom.*

**Can you speak on freedom?**

*I want all to feel the freedom to fully explore their version of the world. That's the beauty of exploration to me: that the starting point is seven billion unique points of view, each coupled with its own unique energies, intentions, perceptions and motivations. The real disaster, to me, is when freedom is restrained in some manner, perhaps religiously, perhaps politically. Then, out of fear, some or many would opt out of exploring the greatness of their unique point of view. This exploration is the aspect of freedom I most love, celebrate and crave.*

**Crave?**

*Yes! I absolutely crave the fun of seeing how far these explorations can go in intriguing, exciting and positive directions, beyond existing levels of being, and beyond those levels, again and again. That's exactly what I crave. Occasionally, I push things along to excite these possibilities.*

*I want to see the next levels of compassion, wisdom and love. I want to see relationships break free of what they are supposed to look like to move to whatever next levels of closeness are possible. I want to see whatever next levels of intimacy are possible. These are qualities of greatness: qualities of me and you that I long to have develop through you, and in so doing, excite humanity to next levels of being in community.*

**How can I help keep this channel open?**

*Remind yourself: I am great pure spirit, greatness of pure light and greatness of pure love. Experience repeatedly the difference between doing this in your head and in your heart. Your heart wants to be connected to the Divine and it wants to be reset whenever that connection is lost. The heart is right there; the breadth and depth of its understanding is there. All you need to do is remember.*

**Sometimes I wish I could just stay within the purity of these divine qualities of greatness. I get tired of falling away from them in order to return.**

*Everything about greatness gets easier and simpler with being in the heart. Complications arise in the mind, and because the mind is what it is, complications will always arise there. Trying to stay connected to the divine through the mind will always require active, conscious effort. Stretching and opening the heart is the way to reside more purely and continuously in greatness.*

*You are already outfitted with divine love that is the attunement of divine greatness. It's like being born with skin: it's a given. This is the real grace of life; it comes unbidden, at the very start of life, and there's nothing to repay. This helps explain why life is so confusing for those who live lives in which exploring greatness seems not to be an option. No matter how walled-off people are from greatness, they are still going to have glimpses of greatness coming their way, or spilling out from them unexpectedly. For many, such moments are just impulses that get pushed back immediately. These glimpses may come in response to drugs or alcohol: glimpses of great fluidity of being, of great connection to others, of great charisma, heart, aliveness, joy, and wisdom that might just come through as, in a moment of being "high," the person touches into his or her core of greatness. Having no access to this state of connectedness becomes increasingly intolerable. He or she may think that substances are required to experience that state. As longing to be back in that space of glimpsing greatness becomes more and more strong, the person might become addicted to the substances.*

*If this can lead to realization that they themselves carry and hold this greatness – that it was there all the time, not contained in the pill, bottle or syringe – the person may be able to realize that the source of greatness is within, not without.*

**Without?**

*There's no harm in being without. Being without is an exploration, just as being within is an exploration, and just as substances like alcohol and drugs are explorations. All these are best when they lead within; at their worst, when they lead to a person becoming more and more lost. If a substance leads you within, and you recognize that place and know that the substance is no longer necessary to arrive there, the whole experience has had a good purpose. Even if it involves great temporary losses, in the end, it leads to greatness that may not have emerged otherwise. When a person uses substances full-time, his body, mind and soul suffer, and others in his life suffer. He is moved further away from a place of greatness by something he has used to help him search for it.*

*Philosophies and beliefs can also serve as outside 'substances' on which we can become reliant. They can be great tools for leading us within, but we have to remember not to substitute them for the actual experience of residing in our own inner greatness. Many spiritual leaders have recognized the grace of greatness within, and this is their most compelling source of communion with their flocks. They recognize that inner experience matters more than the outside scaffolding of religious texts and arcane observances. Without compelling inner experience as a guide, any religious philosophy becomes empty, leaving people hungry.*

*Fortunately, most people find their way within on their own – often, despite their traditions and philosophies. You see: it's inevitable.*

**Inevitable?**

*Imagine my joy every time the universe cracks open and releases yet another person into their true spiritual journey – which is precisely what we've been talking about. It is ecstatic for me to see people turn away from living the life of who they thought they were or who they were supposed to be, and towards who they really are. The glorious truth is that whether in this lifetime or another, every single being comes into this exploration of what is possible.*

**Do you ever get tired of waiting?**

*You have no idea how impatient I am! Much more than you'd*

*ever think. That's precisely why I shake things up, and there are a couple of ways I do that. One is to get out of the way and let people's own choices lead them to the consequences of what will re-attune them to their new journey. If their anger creates a situation where they see what's truly important or if an accident opens their eyes – as tragic as that might be – it might jump-start a few of them into looking at life differently. If that is the case, then no matter how tragic the episode, it is also a momentous occasion where some beings find a beginning point for their true explorations.*

*I might push people off the precipice into facing who they really are through experiences that engage the soul and call for them to revisit the best of who they are. That can be anything from natural disasters to political crises; from Woodstock to watershed elections. All these dramatic moments are geared to show the light to those who are ready for it. For some, the launch has to be harsh and lasting – a great loss, perhaps – to match the need for propulsion out of the old ways of being.*

*If you're going on a journey, at some point, you have to leave the station. When this comes through adversity, I feel bad; but in the same breath, I'm celebrating.*

*Once those who venture into this exploration unfold into its joy and its gratification, they usually only need a few gentle nudges to stay on track. Day by day, they are drawn deeper into the mysteries that surround us all.*

*I am that all. You and all others are part of me. Every time another new person realizes this, I feel joy. Every time someone goes from realization to crystallization – where they begin to live from this realization – I am ecstatic. The energy I am made of dances. I rejoice! I am the energy of love, of greatness, of grace – of all the great qualities. When someone explores the energy of even one quality of greatness, the cosmic orchestra sounds that much better. There is that much more resonance. And when even one person comes into confluence with my energy on many such levels, they begin to attract the attention of those around them. Whether on a local stage or the world stage, they captivate and compel others to explore their own greatness.*

*I have come to realize that I can't do this alone. I can't count on enough people becoming sufficiently awakened by the greatness of my love or my creations to then explore the inspiration of their own greatness. Sadly, I cannot count on that, even as I attempt to heighten beauty and increase love. So I rely on all of you.*

*No level of grace, love, or inspiration alone will accomplish my mission and purpose with so many. My impatience presses me to play with the alchemy of circumstances. My suffering and sadness come with trusting that I am doing the right thing when I create a motivating situation that is harsh – when grace, mystery, and gentle inspiration have failed. I come face-to-face with suffering often under these circumstances. But when even one person shifts as a result of being in the world, renewed – and even more, when a multitude makes this shift – the benefit to the world far outweighs the pain. I have never come away thinking that it wasn't worth all the broken buildings or broken hearts.*

*A broken heart is nothing compared to a renewed heart. A broken heart leads to an open heart, which leads to renewal, which leads to every horizon worth seeking: horizons of peace, love, compassion, understanding, playfulness, giving, receiving, sharing, and inspiration.*

*This may be hard for you to understand: this seemingly purposeful breaking of hearts. But you see how much light can be created this way.*

**Is there a price you pay for that?**

*Absolutely. My suffering can be unbearable when a child or mother dies or when any other losses occur. I feel the pain of all those who experience those losses. It's heart-wrenching. I would much rather be a party purely to grace; a watcher of explorations that are largely self-motivated, with the occasional gentle nudge toward a new edge of greatness.*

*You bear a parallel experience in your own life. You would rather never again need even a molecule of negativity as motivator; but you also know that even if you fully, devotedly bask in light and positivity, there are times when a negative outside or internal event has to arise to create great gains. I often feel in you the most subtle negativity, which draws me to you to interact in a way that quiets the noise, the irritation, the headache. I come to you in those moments to intercede with something designed to reset you. So: if you are subtly ruminating on negativity – not in the middle of consciously using negativity as a motivator toward more greatness, which is my favorite solution, always a win-win – I am drawn to you out of a desire to make that horrible, un-productive 'buzz' go away. I might distract you with beauty or with grace; but most often, I match this quiet buzz of negativity with even greater negativity. It works a little like a homeopathic remedy. Like amplifies like until it triggers a reset in you.*

*Some people get the hang of this quickly – how their negative thoughts fuel amplified negative thoughts and actions, and that a shift is needed. My nudging doesn't always work. Some don't see what I try to make so obvious. It's not from lack of trying. And you thought I had all the powers in the world!*

*If I were you – and I am – I would get to know me by enjoying my experience of your explorations. That would tell you everything about me: how much I love you, how excited I am by your every acquisition, by every molecular move you make in the direction of greatness; and by the way you create consequences in your life that impact your responses in the direction of goodness and greatness.*

*Greatness is a field of energy that always was and always will be in total support of the exploration of all that is sacred. That exploration is endless. It opens doors to ecstasy, fulfillment, joy, and the sharing of a life of love. When we choose with discernment what fits self and others from the integrity of energetic alignment, rather than from limiting views of good and bad based in dogmatic political or traditional beliefs, we are truly free, regardless of the influences that surround us. We come into our own.*

**What does this mean – "come into your own?"**

*It means owning or owning up to your greatness. It means admitting that we possess a divine inheritance that most people have either disowned or projected onto a deity. The wealth in this is staggering.*

*Think of all the lottery winners who falter because they don't have the inner wealth to support their outer wealth. Most have not been in any process of building their inner forms to ready themselves for great earnings. So: gaining great wealth with incongruent timing ends up overwhelming these people's lives, even when it is something they have fervently wished for. By creating inner wealth, you prepare yourself to welcome material wealth, should it come to you. Whether or not it does, you will be balanced, true to yourself, and humanitarian in your use of any wealth you acquire. You'll live a life of love.*

**Can you say more about "a life of love?***"*

*A life of love is the openness to the energy of greatness. It's an appreciation of this energy that is pervasive, and a willingness to dance with, enjoy, and participate in this energy. Participation means willingness to give and take this energy as it comes your way, and to be willing to show and share it as it builds in your heart. Your heart is your GPS, and if you miss a turn, it will tell you how to get back on track.*

*A commitment to a life of love means turning on the GPS in your heart, and to keep tuning and turning up its sensitivity and frequency. It is not about committing to an arbitrary contract to love forever, for better or worse, but rather an ongoing monitoring of the heart. This GPS will naturally lead you deeper into the territory of love; and at each step, your greatness will be altered and expanded.*

*The greatness of love eclipses and alters many other aspects of greatness. Finding greater love makes you want to work out issues that arise, and makes you want to be supportive and encouraging when problems emerge. Staying with love means living not by the letter of a contract, but from within.*

*A life of love can't help but unfold in increasingly deep ways. It always leads back to more of the same.*

*To live a life of love, breathe with your heart and keep the GPS running.*

Wherever this download came from, it tells a story about the loving universe discovering itself through us. It casts adversity as opportunity and encourages us to take note of small, gentle nudges toward greatness and away from negativity, rather than waiting for the more cataclysmic reminders that the loving universe provides where necessary. This is a story that begs a pivotal question for me: if the Universe discovers the Universe and all that is possible though us, then how far can that greatness be taken? How great can the many-splendored realms of greatness become? What are the implications for you and I – what are our roles? What are our real jobs in not only resetting, which to me implies a returning to what was and to the status quo, but also in *renewing* to what lies ahead? What is being urged to unfold by the gentle nudges and the less-than-gentle shoves into next iterations of existence?

What *new* iterations of ourselves can we discover by using our life force in concert with the growing pains and joys of it all? If I am correct that we have all essentially signed up for some version of that, then we can do more than just reset to positivity. We can *renew* to a constantly expanding exploration of what's possible via our unique signatures of intensity and brilliance.

As you explore, hold in your awareness that the Universe discovers the Universe – and, perhaps, we all discover how far we all can go - through *our* explorations. Where are *you* going to set your sights? What purposeful realms of greatness resonate in your life? What greatness are you exploring and pioneering?

# God as
# Greatness

This practice can be opened up to people of all belief systems with this syllogism: If God is great, and I wish to pray to God, then my prayer honoring the sacredness of spirit is essentially to greatness.

The greatness of God is universally accepted, but it seems hard for us to accept our own greatness. In some faith traditions, it is customary to praise God in highly specific terms. Quite a few ancient faiths, for example, reverently honor the one hundred names of God. These are almost all, at their root, qualities of greatness. What if we were to all recognize these qualities in ourselves? This would not be a minimizing of the greatness of God, if that is part of our belief system; it is a way of seeing ourselves in God, and of seeing God in ourselves.

Part of my personal practice, along with my reverence for spirit and all that is sacred, is in choosing to pray (or praise, or 'prayze') to specific qualities of greatness that help me to feel and explore the global concept of greatness in increasingly accessible ways and ways that will be of service to the great good.

As deftly as we can attribute greatness to the divine, the average person struggles to accept attributes of his or her own greatness. Awakening as many people as I can to their own greatness is my mission and purpose. Frankly, I've never been nearly as riveted, fascinated or compelled on a daily basis by anything before or since. I've made this my daily practice for nearly fifteen years and unceasingly felt compelled to see how far I can take it. How far can I expand the depth and breath of my experience? As I've played with this, I sometimes feel myself moving mountains on the inside – and concurrently, multiple mountains seem to move before my eyes.

Recognition of your own greatness happens as you become aware of the constant unfolding of individual and compound qualities of greatness in the Now. Its presence is a given: it's all been there the whole time, waiting for your recognition to bring it to life. All you need to do is discern it and enjoy it. Even while experiencing difficulties and challenging emotions, you can use the enormous energy of these experiences and emotions to provide trajectories of greatness above and beyond the ordinary.

Even if your life has been challenging to this point, and even if it feels challenging this very second, you are indeed already *'being greatness.'*

Even if the kindling is wet, so to speak, and the fire is hard to start, once it gets going the fire takes on a life of its own, and you will find you are *living* greatness and *standing* in greatness. Fan the spark until it catches.

Keep feeding it. At a certain point, simply breathing into the fire will be enough to build it into a bonfire of greatness.

Instead of the winds being a deterrent, they propel and fuel this fire of greatness. Rain cannot extinguish this kind of fire. It brightens every person and every situation and can be seen from miles around. This very fire will be the one you carry within. It will warm you and others from the inside out. I have come to love the heat, the radiance and the luminosity of that fire.

For me, the fire began with those lightning strikes I mentioned in the first part of this book, and has been brought to brighter life over time through dedicated use of the techniques of appreciation of the Nurtured Heart Approach. I wasn't thinking or speaking in terms of greatness in the beginning, but at some point, it began to surface, and kept doing so, insistently. That simple word seemed to multiply the impact of what I was honing and achieving.

When I worked up the courage to share this at a training of trainers, I did so gingerly, not knowing how it would be received. I knew that the word "greatness" tended to raise defenses. People didn't have a hard time seeing themselves as *good*. But *great?* I feared it would feel like hubris to many, and for those who believed in a higher power, I could see some conflict in equating themselves with qualities they would normally attribute to that higher power.

At the next break, out in the lobby, I overheard conversation after conversation among participants honoring the greatness that had been recognized and expressed. At that moment, I saw how this word, *greatness,* and its particular use in this approach, was now officially out of control. Once shared, it was irretrievable. And in light of the many negative ways people or ideas can spin out and do damage, I saw that this was an amazing and desirable way to be out of control!

This is not a game of hide-and-seek; you already are everything you wish to be; owning and polishing these qualities will serve to alter the trajectory of living these qualities, but know that they are already within you right this moment. As you enter a space of being your greatness, everything around you begins to manifest in relation to this aspect of your being. You attract others who are living their greatness.

If there is a God you choose to worship, know that you are seeing in them a reflection of your own greatness. Any quality you see in your God, you can claim as your own, and you can expand it through loving acknowledgement and attention. That quality is in you, and it can be propelled. As you engage in this sacred work/play of building greatness, you come to live fully in love.

# About the
# Authors

## Howard Neil Glasser

Howard Glasser is the Chairman of the Board of the Children's Success Foundation and creator of The Nurtured Heart Approach®. He is dedicated to awakening the greatness in all children, with a particular focus on intense and challenging children.

The approach's core methodologies, born out of his extensive clinical work, effectively inspire difficult children to successfully channel their intensity. Worldwide, hundreds of thousands of parents, educators, and treatment and child-advocacy agencies have used this approach with consistently transformative results.

Howard is the author of Transforming the Difficult Child, currently the top-selling book on ADHD; Notching Up the Nurtured Heart Approach: The New Inner Wealth Initiative, a leading book on school interventions; and All Children Flourishing, on using the NHA with all children, difficult or not. He is currently working on his latest release, entitled Igniting Greatness.

Four of Howard's eight books are in the top one percent of all books on Amazon, confirming the need and relevance of his message and methodology. All parents and educators, even those with well-behaved children, can benefit from learning how to inspire thriving relationships through the Nurtured Heart Approach®.

Howard has been called one of the most influential living persons working to reduce children's reliance on psychiatric medications. His work also supports children in resisting addictive substances. He has been a featured guest on CNN, a consultant for 48 Hours, and was recently featured in Esquire. He currently instructs educators, parents and therapists through live presentations and Internet-based courses.

Although he has done extensive doctoral work in Clinical Psychology and Educational Leadership, he credits his own years as an intense child as the strongest contributors to his understanding of the needs of children with immense life force.

## Melissa Lynn Lowenstein

Melissa Lowenstein (formerly Block) is an author and editor who has collaborated on seven books with Howard Glasser. She is also a Nurtured Heart trainer; a facilitator and grant writer for the AHA! (Attitude. Harmony. Achievement.) program for teens, which brings social-emotional learning to 3500 youth each year in southern California; a parent and stepparent; and has been, over the years, a yoga teacher, contemporary dancer and choreographer, visual artist, theater director and actor, and enthusiastic participant in personal growth groups and workshops.

She lives in Santa Barbara, California with her partner, William Swan, her two school-aged children, and Will's teen son. She loves to read, write in her journal, watch great films, and spend time outdoors near bodies of water and very large trees.

# Nurtured Heart
# Approach Resources

**Online Classes and Support**

The Children's Success Foundation website:
www.ChildrensSuccessFoundation.com is the online learning
center for the Nurtured Heart Approach. There, parents,
educators, coaches and therapists can learn about the approach
and then continually hone their expertise through innovative
web courses, learning modules, discussion forums, and NHA-
related research. The site also features articles, products and
services supporting the approach.

**Books on the Nurtured Heart Approach**

Books can also be ordered online through Amazon.com or
through the Nurtured Heart Approach Bookstore at
www.ChildrensSuccessFoundation.com. Phone orders can be
made toll free by calling our fulfillment center, SPExpress:
(800) 311-3132.

Transforming the Difficult Child: The Nurtured Heart Approach
(Revised 2013) by Howard Glasser and Jennifer Easley

Transforming the Difficult Child WORKBOOK—An Interactive
Guide to the Nurtured Heart Approach (2013) by Howard
Glasser, Joann Bowdidge and Lisa Bravo

All Children Flourishing—Igniting the Greatness of Our
Children (2008) by Howard Glasser with Melissa Lynn Block

Transforming the Difficult Child: True Stories of Triumph (2008) by Howard Glasser and Jennifer Easley

ADHD Without Drugs—A Guide to the Natural Care of Children with ADHD (2010) by Sanford Newmark, MD

Notching Up the Nurtured Heart Approach—The New Inner Wealth Initiative for Educators (2011) Howard Glasser and Melissa Lynn Block

Notching Up the Nurtured Heart Approach WORKBOOK— The New Inner Wealth Initiative for Educators (2011) Lisa Bravo with Melissa Lynn Block

**Audio Visual Resources**

Transforming the Difficult Child DVD—(2004) 6 hours based on an actual filmed one-day seminar, with video clip illustrations

Transforming the Difficult Child DVD—(2004) 4 hours based on an abbreviated version of the above

Transforming the Difficult Child CD—(2011) 3.5 hours recorded from a live seminar

Transforming the Difficult Child: The Nurtured Heart Approach—Audio Book (2012)—by Howard Glasser and Jennifer Easley, read by Howard Glasser

Other titles by Nurtured Heart Approach trainers can be found at the Nurtured Heart Approach bookstore.